# SECRET
# OMAHA

## A Guide to the Weird, Wonderful, and Obscure

*Ryan Roenfeld*

Library of Congress Control Number: 2020950054

ISBN: 9781681063065

Design by Jill Halpin
All image are courtesy of the author unless otherwise noted.

Printed in the United States of America
20 21 22 23 24  5 4 3 2 1

To the people of Omaha

Special thanks to my family and co-workers, Amanda Pokorski, Michaela Armetta, Shannon Lewis, Harl and Kay Calame Dalstrom, Greg Jerrett; the fine staff at Reedy Press; and Adam, Jody, Micah, Michelle, Jill, and the other administrators and members of The Omaha History Club on Facebook.

# CONTENTS

1 ................................................................................. Introduction

2 ............................................................................... Omaha Blues

4 .............................................................. Little Italy's Giant Fork

6 ................................................................... Site of the Civic

8 .......................................................... A Garden with the Zodiac

10 ................................................................ An Explosion over Dundee

12 ................................................................... Millard Sky Park

14 ................................................................ The Omaha Platform

16 ................................................................ Get Scalped and Survive

18 ................................................................. The Best View of Omaha

20 ........................................................... Alone in the Missouri

22 ................................................................ Aristotle in Omaha

24 ................................................... The Statue Saved from a Ditch

26 ......................................................... A Memorial to Central Elementary

28 ............................................................ Benson and Its Bunnies

30 ................................................................ Rosenfield's Peonies

32 .................................................................. The Bloody Corner

34 ................................................................ Omaha's "Prettiest Mile"

36 ...................................................................... Preserving Some Prairie

38 ........................................................... A Roller Coaster Disaster

40 .................................................... John O'Neill, the Hero of Ridgeway

42 ........................................................... A Painting Attacked Twice

44 ............................................................ Who Killed Harry Lapidus?

46 ................................................................ Beadle's Rock Brook Claim

48 ............................................................................... Minne Lusa

50 ................................................................ Some Copenhagen in Omaha

52 ............................................................. The Elmwood Grotto

54 ................................... The Murder at the University of Omaha

56 ............................................................................ Sheelytown

58 ................................................... Walk with Standing Bear

60 ................................................................... That Florence Bank

62 ......................................... Union Pacific Shop Yards Monument

64 ................................................................................ Goose Hollow

66 ................................................................... Cut-Off Island

68 ........................................................................ Hummel Park

70 ............................... A German Prince and George Washington

72 ............................................................... The Original Omaha

74 ...................................................... Only Governor for Two Days

76 ...................................................................... The Golden Spike

78 ................................................... The General in a Garden

80 ............................................................ Site of Courtland Beach

82 ................................................................ The Military Road

84 ............................................................................... ASARCO

86 ...................................................... California Street

106 .................................................... Lowering the Streets

108 ........................................................................ The Florence Mill

110 .............................. Omaha's Expositions and Indian Congress

112 ..................................................................... Winter Quarters

114 .............................................................. The Greektown Riot

116 ........................................................................ The Prague Hotel

118 ...................................................... A Pabst Tied House

120 ............................................. Scars of the 1919 Courthouse Riot

122 ............................................................................ Brandeis

124 .........................................................Potter's Field

126 ..........................................The Otoe Mission

128 ...................................... Omaha's Main Street

130 ............................. The Blockhouse and Mission

132 .............................................................DeBolt

134 ............................... Monuments to Stockyards

136 ..................................The Iowa School for the Deaf

138 ...................................... Depot on the Omaha Road

140 ................................... The Gangster and the Architect

142 ...................................Marker for the Mainline

144 ....................................Ak-Sar-Ben Air Field

146 ........................ Futurism, Bicycles, and Coffee

148 .......................................... Cutler's Park

150 ..................................Resting Place of the Omaha Kid

152 ........................ The Byron Reed Numismatic Collection

154 ...............................Mr. Blandings's Dream Home

156 ...............................The Singing Tower of Westlawn

158 .......................................... Everything at the Center

160 .......................................... Last Home of the Tong

162 ...................................... The *Tägliche Omaha Tribüne*

164 ...................................................................... Gibson

166 ......................................... Home of an Ice Baron

168 ...........................................................Druid Hall

170 ......................................... Site of the St. Nicholas

172 ...................................The Last of Jobber's Canyon

174 ......................................... Omaha's First Skyscraper

176 ..............................................................The Farmers Home

178 ................................................... A Park for Survivors

180 ............................................................. Big Elk

182 ................................................ Hell's Half Acre

184 ............................................. Dundee Streetcars

186 ................................... Around the World to Omaha

188 ..................................................... Sources

198 ......................................................... Index

# INTRODUCTION

On the banks of the Big Muddy Missouri River a city was founded in 1854 that would become the metropolis of a state. It was born as both a Western dream and mercenary speculation that made some rich, left others dead, and provided a load of intriguing stories and strange sites along the way. The completion of the transcontinental railroad in 1869 only cemented the city's importance on the edge of the Great Plains. One 2018 estimate gave the city a population of 468,000 with a surrounding metropolitan population rapidly approaching one million. Long-time locals might never have heard of some of these places or passed by others a million times without noticing. For visitors, this is the opportunity to see just some of what makes Omaha such a unique place.

Unlike the typical Midwestern city, Omaha didn't spread outward in easy and growing concentric rings. Instead, the city moved west with the country, annexing a variety of other once-independent towns along the way. Places like South Omaha, Florence, Dundee, Benson, and Millard may all be legally part of Omaha today but each one has preserved its own unique character. At the same time, near downtown sits a small Iowa town of only a few thousand with the Iowa city of Council Bluffs on the east bank of the river. In Omaha, Military Avenue originated as the 1857 US Army route west to Fort Kearney with a long local history of Native Americans and Missouri River fur traders. There are quaint shops in the Old Market and quaint shops on Main Street even though the two places are over 15 miles apart, with one near 10th Street and the other out near 205th. There are many more secrets to uncover in Omaha, and if you'd like to share any of those that you find just tweet #Secret_Omaha to @Secret_Omaha.

# OMAHA BLUES

## Where did the music play all night?

Joseph Lee Williams—known by everyone as Big Joe—was born near Nuxobee Swamp in Mississippi in 1903. Big Joe's story was that of the classic itinerant bluesman who left home young to play guitar wherever he could. Williams was known for his signature nine-string guitar and songs of sorrow, boasting, booze, and pain. In the 1930s he recorded "Baby, Please Don't Go" and "Crawlin' King Snake," both of which have gone on to become blues standards. It isn't known when or why he was in or out of Omaha or exactly what was up with his cousin Melinda. Something about the place must have stayed with him. In 1958, Williams recorded the song "Omaha Blues," revealing an easy familiarity with the intersection of 24th and Lake Streets, the heart of Omaha's Black business district during the 20th century.

Historically, the 24th and Lake Historic District was better known for its jazz. The Dreamland, the Carnation, Allen's Showcase, and other venues brought touring musicians through

### 24TH AND LAKE

**What:** An intersection with its own song.

**Where:** 24th and Lake Sts.

**Cost:** Free to visit during daylight hours.

**Pro Tip:** Find out more about Omaha's musical legacy at the Love's Jazz Center at 2510 N. 24th St. and the Great Plains Black History Museum at the Jewell Building at 2221 N. 24th St.

The sculpture *Jazz Trio* by Littleton Alston at the Dreamland Plaza at North 24th and Lizzie Robinson Avenue just south of Lake.

*The southeast corner of 24th and Lake Streets and the sculpture* Jazz Trio.

and made the city a hotbed of musical activity as home base for "territory bands" run by Lloyd Hunter, Dan Desdunes, and others whose orchestras toured the Midwest. Big Joe Williams kept playing and found some measure of fame during the 1960s folk revival. He died in 1982. The song's last line says he'll be back in Omaha some sunny day but it remains unknown if he ever made it.

# LITTLE ITALY'S GIANT FORK

## How can a sculpture be served al dente?

There's a giant fork in the hills south of downtown that commemorates an immigrant enclave whose traditions continue to this day. The slanted neighborhood built through the river bluffs was a haven for Italian immigrants during the late 19th and early 20th centuries. At one time, there were four separate enclaves of Italian immigrants around the city but this one is the best known today. Work was available in the nearby Union Pacific Railroad shop yards and Little Italy provided a welcoming neighborhood full of friends and family from home.

It was the Salerno brothers, Joseph and Sebastiano, who were responsible for bringing so many Sicilians to Omaha where the population of Italian immigrants skyrocketed. There were only some 450 Italians in Omaha in 1900, mostly Calabrese clustered around South 24th Street and Poppleton Avenue near the site of St. Ann's Catholic Church. It was in 1904 when Sebastiano Salerno became an agent for a steamship company while his brother worked to find the new immigrants jobs and housing in the hilly neighborhood south of downtown still known as Little Italy. By 1908 there were 2,000 Italian immigrants in Omaha, almost all from Carlentini in Sicily or nearby Calabria at the end of Italy's boot. One long-lasting

A true neighborhood landmark, Orsi's Bakery at 621 Pacific Street was opened by World War I veteran Alfonso Orsi in 1919, and their fresh bread and Sicilian-style pizza still draw crowds after a century.

*Fork with spaghetti.*

## A LITTLE ITALY LANDMARK

**What:** A 13-foot-tall stainless steel fork with pasta

**Where:** 1115 S. 7th St.

**Cost:** Free to view during daylight hours.

**Pro Tip:** Cascio's Steakhouse at 1620 S. 10th St. is one of the last of Omaha's classic Italian steakhouses.

tradition in the Little Italy neighborhood is the annual Santa Lucia festival that originated in 1924. Grazia Bonafede Caniglia is credited with the design for the representation of Santa Lucia that was made in Italy and paid for with donations from the neighborhood. The annual event is still held today and to commemorate Little Italy's rich heritage the Homeowners Association commissioned Omaha artist Jake Balcom. The result stands today as the *Stile di Famiglia*.

# SITE OF THE CIVIC

## Who won the 1988 vice-presidential debate?

At present, there is only a massive lot awaiting development at a place that was once the site of hundreds of high school and college graduations and rodeos and car shows and music concerts. These events are now held at the CHI Health Center Arena, but from 1954 until 2014, Omahans attended all sorts of events at the Civic Auditorium or the attached Mancusco Music Hall. Elvis Presley played one of his final concerts there, which was filmed for a CBS television special. The Clash played there too, and the annual Boat and Travel Show was a mainstay. One of the Flying Wallendas died during a trapeze act at the Civic, and the Rolling Stones played there on their first American concert tour. There were the Grateful Dead, Prince, and KISS. There was Ozzy Osbourne with Mötley Crüe as the opening act, and there were Tom Petty, The Ramones, REM, Rush, Marilyn Manson with Nine Inch Nails, Fleetwood Mac, and the Eagles. Yes, the Civic hosted both Omaha-born Malcolm X in 1964 and segregationist politician George Wallace, whose inflammatory speech helped spark the city's 1968 race riot. Still, the site's true significance might come from a quip made during the 1988 vice-presidential debate. It was at the Civic Auditorium in October 1988 when Lloyd Bentsen gave Dan Quayle the zinger of all time and sternly told the future vice-president in front of the whole world, "Senator, you're no Jack Kennedy." Pundits

The CHI Health Center at 455 North 10th Street first opened in 2003 and was originally known as the Qwest Center Omaha.

*The 2020 view looking south along North 17th Street towards Capitol Avenue.*

everywhere reeled, although the Dukakis and Bentsen ticket would go down to defeat the next month. Nevertheless, the phrase is still used to this day whenever a politician needs to be taken down a peg.

## I SAW IT AT THE CIVIC

**What:** Site of the Omaha Civic Auditorium

**Where:** The lot bounded by Capitol Ave. and Chicago St. from 17th west to 19th St.

**Cost:** Free to visit during daylight hours.

**Pro Tip:** Go to www. chihealthcenteromaha.com for the latest schedule of upcoming concerts and events.

# A GARDEN WITH THE ZODIAC

## What's behind that door?

There's an art gallery of rotating exhibits tucked away in Omaha's Old Market Passageway. In the back, there's a door that opens on a vine-entangled garden that offers something unexpected. This art garden features the sculptures of Swiss artist Eva Aeppli. The Garden of the Zodiac is arranged around the location of the signs of the constellations in the sky on the day of the artist's 1925 birth. Aeppli's unique take on the traditional representations of the signs of the zodiac can be both striking and unexpected.

The design of the garden came from Sam Mercer. It was Mercer's vision that made the Old Market a reality, sort of by way of London and Paris. Sam Mercer's grandfather was Dr. Sam Mercer, a Civil War veteran who came to Omaha in 1866 and prospered in real estate, streetcars, and more. He worked to open the city's first hospital, was the chief surgeon for the Union Pacific Railroad, and was among those who started building speculative warehouses in what became the Old Market. His grandson and namesake Sam was born in London in 1924. He grew up in both Omaha and London, where he was educated in law. However, Paris was where Sam Mercer would end up spending most of his time. As the years passed, the old warehouse district where Mercer's family had invested faded away as the neighborhood seemed destined to be razed.

*The Garden during the summer.*

Instead, Sam Mercer transformed it into something else. In 1969, Mercer helped open the French Cafe with real live chefs from Paris and urban apartments upstairs. That was something new in a city of steakhouses and subdivisions, especially in the heart of a run-down neighborhood of crumbling brick streets and buildings. Then came Mr. Toad's Pub, art galleries, and head shops along with bohemians. There's a small memorial for Mercer in the garden and around it is a lively neighborhood instead of a sea of parking.

The Old Market's Passageway also includes shops, restaurants, and the *Fountain of Erinnyesdiac*, another unique art display by Eva Aeppli.

# AN EXPLOSION OVER DUNDEE

## How far can a balloon bomb fly?

No look at Omaha oddities could leave out the time toward the end of World War II when the Japanese Empire bombed the Dundee neighborhood with a Fu-Go, a bomb carried by a balloon. That streetcar suburb was originally an upper-class haven of strict covenants that was established outside the official city limits of rowdy Omaha. After annexation into Omaha, Dundee evolved into an eclectic neighborhood of beautiful homes, winding streets, and a tradition of toney ambiance unlike elsewhere in the city. It was on April 18, 1945, that a balloon bomb exploded in the sky over 50th Street and Underwood Avenue. It happened at night and made a pretty sight but thankfully caused no damage or injury. The war against the Japanese Empire ended just over four months later.

That balloon bomb was just one of thousands of similar devices deployed by the Japanese Empire. The balloons were released up into the jet stream to be carried east across the Pacific Ocean. If things went according to plan, this would result in widespread forest fires and random terror across the western United States.

Instead, the balloon bombs mostly didn't go according to plan, although a woman and five children were killed in Oregon in May 1945. At the time, the government apparently stifled

---

**THE DUNDEE BALLOON BOMB**

**What:** Marker commemorating WWII balloon bomb attack.

**Where:** 5003 Underwood Ave.

**Cost:** Free to view during daylight hours

**Pro Tip:** The Dundee-Happy Hollow Historic District was listed on the National Register of Historic Places in 1995.

*The Harte Block at North 50th Street and Underwood Avenue.*

accounts of these strange explosions and random fires to avoid panic, and only a few hundred of the estimated 6,000 balloon bombs sent across the Pacific Ocean have ever been officially accounted for. The most recent was discovered in 2019 in British Columbia, Canada. The marker for the Dundee explosion was dedicated in 1992.

The nearby Memorial Park at 6005 Underwood Avenue was dedicated by President Harry S. Truman in 1948.

# MILLARD SKY PARK

## How can you live right next to an airport?

In the 1960s, it seemed like everything would be possible in the distant future—Americans might even jump into their private planes and sail away into the sky for work and pleasure. With that in mind, one interesting stretch of the Millard Heights development included a specially designed and designated "Sky Park." This was just southwest of the Millard airport, with 23 lots specifically intended for a different sort of home. From the front, the houses would seem little different than any others in the middle-class neighborhood. However, these homes would feature their own hangars in the back with a private taxiway straight into the adjacent airport and up into to sky. After all, Millard's slogan was the "City of Progress."

The future must have seemed bright. That small stop along the Union Pacific Railroad line still only had 400 people in the early 1950s. Then came the opening of a sprawling Western Electric plant on a 390-acre campus, and things changed fast. Farmland was soon replaced by new

## AN AIRPORT NEIGHBORHOOD

**What:** A neighborhood designed for airplanes.

**Where:** The homes are along Sky Park Dr., and the Millard Airport is at S. 132nd and Z Sts.

**Cost:** Free to view during daylight hours

**Pro Tip:** The small Millard Heights Park at the eastern end of Sky Park Circle is a nice place to watch airplanes.

The independent spirit of the former town continues to be celebrated in the annual Millard Days.

*Homes along Sky Park Drive.*

housing developments, including the Sky Park. By 1970, Millard's population had exploded to 7,460. After that, as with Florence, Dundee, and South Omaha before, the City of Omaha proposed annexation. The contentious feud over annexation made its way to the Nebraska Supreme Court, and some Millard residents hung Omaha Mayor Eugene Leahy in effigy. The court ruled against Millard, and the former town was annexed in 1971. Security concerns eventually ended the private entrances to the airport in what still remains a unique sort of neighborhood development.

# THE OMAHA PLATFORM

## Where did the radicals all meet?

There is little remarkable today along this stretch of North 20th Street, and nothing marks or commemorates this unique political happening in American history. From 1889 to 1927, this was the site of the Ak-Sar-Ben Den Coliseum. In 1892, the Den hosted the political convention for the newly formed "Populist" People's Party. The convention was held in July and attracted radicals and reformers from across the nation who were trying to forge an alliance between rural farmers and industrialized workers in the cities. They worked together to create a new progressive political party free of both Democrats and Republicans. They came together at North 20th and Burdette Streets in Omaha to create what they wanted to be the second Declaration of Independence.

This was the Omaha Platform that attempted to reform a country where, for some, neither political party offered any choice at all. The preamble to the new document was written by Minnesota politician Ignatius Donnelly, who is best remembered today for his odd theories concerning ancient civilizations,

"Jumping Jim" Weaver earned his nickname for running as a candidate for the Republican, Greenback, Populist, and Democratic parties.

*The west side of North 20th Street is now the home of The Hope Center for Kids Omaha.*

Atlantis, and who really wrote *Romeo and Juliet*. The document included such radical demands as the direct election of United States Senators, a graduated income tax, public ownership of utilities and railroads, and increasing the value of silver in comparison to gold. The convention also nominated Civil War General James Weaver of Bloomfield, Iowa, as its candidate for president. That fall, Weaver received over a million votes and 22 electoral votes as one of America's most successful third-party candidates. Some (though not all) of the ideas in the Omaha Platform are popular today. The Ak-Sar-Ben Den burned in 1927, and the North Omaha Gene Eppley Boys' Club was built on the site in 1962.

# GET SCALPED AND SURVIVE

## Would you pay to see the man who got scalped?

There's a truly unique artifact housed at Omaha's downtown W. Dale Clark Library: the scalp of William Thompson. If that seems a strange item for an urban library to exhibit, the story of how it found its way there is just as interesting. Thompson was an English immigrant who was working for the Union Pacific Railroad out of Omaha. The transcontinental railroad still wasn't completed in August 1867 when Thompson and a crew of men were sent to repair a cut telegraph line west of present-day Lexington, Nebraska. The men were out on the Great Plains when they were met by members of the Cheyenne Nation, and what resulted was the Plum Creek Railroad Attack. No one is exactly sure what happened during the encounter, and no one likely ever asked the Cheyenne. They spoke an Algonquian language and were in Minnesota when American westward expansion pushed them farther west. There they took up the horse and hunting buffalo on the grasslands. The railroad being built across the Great Plains would alter their lives forever, and there was really nowhere else left for them to move.

During the Plum Creek attack, William Thompson was shot and then scalped and left for dead. He either woke up with the scalp still beside him, or else he somehow found a way to get it back. He took it to an Omaha doctor in the hope that

An account of the Plum Creek Railroad Attack appeared in the September 7, 1867 issue of *Harper's Weekly*.

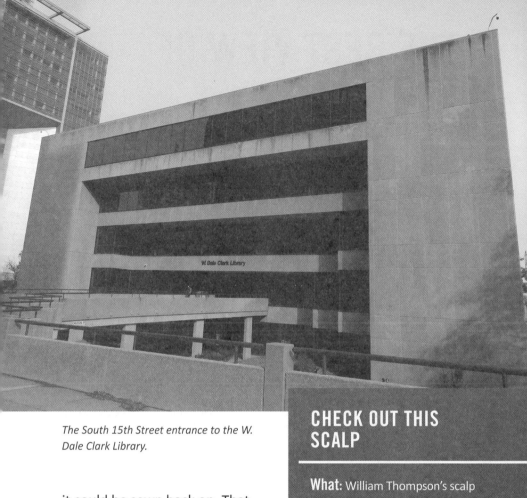

*The South 15th Street entrance to the W. Dale Clark Library.*

it could be sewn back on. That didn't work. So Thompson did what anyone would do—he had it tanned and went back to England to charge money to see the man who had been scalped and lived. He later sent the scalp back to the Omaha doctor, who donated it to the library.

## CHECK OUT THIS SCALP

**What:** William Thompson's scalp

**Where:** The W. Dale Clark Library at 215 S. 15th St.

**Cost:** Check https://omahalibrary.org/locations/OD/ for current hours.

**Pro Tip:** The scalp is only available by appointment.

# THE BEST VIEW OF OMAHA

## Where does the West really begin?

The best view of Omaha's skyline might just be from the Loess Hills of Council Bluffs, Iowa. Near a historic cemetery at the top of Lafayette Avenue, there's a turn-out and commemorative column that provides a commanding view west across the river valley toward Omaha. The historical marker at the site was dedicated in 1911 to honor the 1859 visit by Abraham Lincoln to the city. Council Bluffs seems as far west as Lincoln ever got, and he arrived on board a Missouri River steamboat. Although not officially running for anything at the time, he surely seemed in town to do a bit of politicking and gave an enthusiastic speech at the city's Concert Hall. Officially, he came to Council Bluffs to examine the collateral on a business proposition with Norman Judd of the Rock Island Railroad.

A few years later, during the Civil War, Abraham Lincoln signed the Pacific Railroad Act to authorize the construction of a railroad west from Council Bluffs. Whether or not Lincoln actually hiked up that hill is historically debatable, but it's hard to argue with the stunning view, particularly at sunrise and sunset. In the days of the Lincoln Highway, the Lincoln Monument became an aptly named landmark for the first tourists in the early days of automobile travel.

---

Daniel Chester French's *Black Angel* sculpture at nearby 623 North 2nd Street is officially known as the Ruth Anne Dodge Memorial.

*The Lincoln Monument on Lafayette Avenue in Council Bluffs, Iowa.*

## THE LINCOLN MONUMENT

**What:** A scenic city view

**Where:** The Lincoln Monument at the head of Lafayette Ave. in Council Bluffs, Iowa

**Cost:** Free to visit during daylight hours

**Pro Tip:** The Lincoln-Fairview Historic District was listed on the National Register of Historic Places in 2007.

# ALONE IN THE MISSOURI

## What happened to the amazing marvels of the past?

There's just one reminder left from what was heralded as the amazing marvel of 1888.

That was when the two cities on opposite banks of the river got together to celebrate the opening of the new Omaha & Council Bluffs Railway bridge. The new bridge was the first alternative to paying the Union Pacific Railroad to cross the river between the two cities. The opening of the new bridge also marked the introduction of electric streetcar service between downtown Council Bluffs and Omaha that would thrive for decades. The new electric streetcars bolstered a sense of metropolitan modernity where cattle still sometimes ran down the street. It was the electric streetcar company that would consolidate a variety of competing transit lines in the two cities to create the Omaha and Council Bluffs Street Railway Company.

That bridge became something more in 1913 when it was part of the official route of the Lincoln Highway between Times Square in New York City and Golden Gate Park in San Francisco. Omaha's Knights of Ak-Sar-Ben purchased the bridge in 1938, and tolls were abolished in 1947. The route over the bridge was still US Highway 6 until 1966 when the new bridge over Interstate 480 opened, and the old bridge was razed. The lone

---

## A BRIDGE PIER

**What:** Remnant of the 1888 O&CB Bridge

**Where:** Best viewed from either the Omaha Riverfront Trail in Omaha or Tom Hanafan River's Edge Park in Council Bluffs

**Cost:** Free to view during daylight hours

**Pro Tip:** Near the pier on the Council Bluffs bank stands the *Big Mo* by sculptor Mark di Suvero.

*The last pier south of the I-480 Missouri River Bridge.*

pier was left, supposedly for a scenic restaurant that was never
built. It remains in the river as a landmark and peculiarity where it
once supported the crossing of a multitude.

From 1913 until 1930 the bridge was the route of
the transcontinental Lincoln Highway.

# ARISTOTLE IN OMAHA

## Where's Shakespeare downtown?

It can seem strange to stumble down Harney Street and look up to see a group of strange faces looking down at you. There's the perhaps mythical and maybe not even blind Greek poet Homer, who is said to have written the *Iliad* and the *Odyssey*. There are the Greek philosophers Aristotle and Socrates, along with the playwright Sophocles. Tragically, of the 120 plays written by Sophocles, only seven survive, including *Antigone* and *Oedipus Rex*. Romans represented include the statesman Cicero, who fought to preserve the Republic until he was put to death; Julius Caesar, who spread Latin all over Europe; and the poet Virgil, who wrote the *Aeneid* as a sequel to the *Odyssey* a couple hundred years later. Under the faces are engraved the names of a variety of authors, including the expected Shakespeare, Milton, and Dante. There are also a few less famous, including the 16th-century Italian poet Torquato Tasso. There are the French writers Jean-Baptiste Poquelin (better known as Molière) and Jean Racine, along with the Germans Friedrich Schiller and Johann Wolfgang von Goethe.

Omaha's old public library first opened in 1894. The building was designed by Omaha architect Thomas Kimball in what would be his first public commission toward the beginning of a lengthy and significant career. The Second Renaissance Revival building mirrors the 1895 Boston Public Library designed by famed architects McKim, Mead, and White. Omaha's old library

## THE OLD LIBRARY

**What:** Friezes of Philosophers

**Where:** 1823 Harney St.

**Cost:** Free to view during daylight hours

**Pro Tip:** The lobby is accessible to the public.

*The 1894 library building on Harney Street.*

closed in 1977 with the opening of the W. Dale Clark Library. The old building was named an Omaha Landmark and listed on the National Register of Historic Places soon afterward, and it was later converted into offices.

The 1906 home Thomas Kimball designed for his mother can still be seen at 2236 St. Mary's Avenue.

# THE STATUE SAVED FROM A DITCH

## Who would vandalize a statue?

He was a poet, historian, and philosopher who died of tuberculosis at the age of 45.

Years after his death, Friedrich Schiller would be held up by German immigrants as a cultural treasure. Today, most people have never heard of him. Schiller was born in 1759 in Marbach am Neckar in what is now southwestern Germany. His 1781 drama *The Robbers* gave Schiller his early fame and notoriety. The story of two brothers was a social critique that questioned just who the real robbers were in this world. To see it on opening night in Mannheim, Schiller left his position as a military doctor at Stuttgart; as a result, he had to serve two weeks in prison. He eventually moved to Weimar in central Germany, married and had two children, was elevated to the nobility, and died in 1805.

Friedrich Schiller never visited Omaha or even the United States. Still, the first statue dedicated in Central Park in New York City in 1859 was in his honor. Later statues appeared in St. Paul and Chicago. In July 1907, in Omaha, some 6,000 people attended the unveiling of the city's monument to Friedrich Schiller at the city's old Riverview Park near the present entrance to the Henry Doorly Zoo at 3701 South 10th Street. However, America's entry into World War I changed how Omaha and America viewed those of German descent. In

The German-American Society originated in 1883 as the Omaha Plattdeutcher Verein by immigrants who spoke the Low German or Plattdeutsche dialect.

*Schiller* at the German-American Society on South 120th Street.

1918, Schiller's statue was first vandalized with yellow paint and then removed and thrown in a nearby ravine. Schiller's bust was saved and was eventually installed at a safer location on the grounds of the German-American Society building, where he now gazes west across the parking lot at South 120th Street.

## STATUE OF SCHILLER

**What:** The rescued statue of a German philosopher

**Where:** 3717 S. 120th St.

**Cost:** Free to view during daylight hours

**Pro Tip:** From Maifest and Oktoberfest to Christmas, please see https://www.germanamericansociety.org/ for upcoming happenings.

25

# A MEMORIAL TO CENTRAL ELEMENTARY

## What can be learned having a seat and watching the world?

Omaha's founders envisioned Nebraska's forever capital at the summit of Capitol Hill, believing that the city would always remain central to everything west of the Missouri River and north of the 40th parallel. That wasn't what exactly happened, and events have left the city's Capitol Avenue somewhat of a misnomer. What happened instead was that Nebraska became a state in 1867 over President Andrew Johnson's veto, and the seat of government was moved out of town.

Instead of Omaha, the capital of the new State of Nebraska was well to the southwest, south of the Platte River, at the village of Lancaster, now called Lincoln. Instead of politics, Capitol Hill became known for education. Omaha architect John Latenser, Sr. designed the present Omaha Central High School building, which was constructed between 1900 and 1912. The building's most recent addition was completed in 2020. On the south side of Dodge Street across from Central High is a small memorial to a different school that's no longer there. A small park now marks the one-time location of Central Elementary School, which first opened in 1893. The school building was razed 82 years later, in 1975. The small memorial

The 19-story skyscraper to the west was constructed during the 1950s for Northern Natural Gas and was briefly the corporate headquarters of the infamous Enron Corporation.

*The site of Central Elementary on Dodge Street.*

includes the front steps as well as some decorative remnants of the building and a small historical marker. There is seating provided for those who want to relax while taking in some of the surroundings or else just recuperate from having hiked up the hill from 16th Street.

## CENTRAL ELEMENTARY

**What:** The Site of Central Elementary

**Where:** On what should be the southeast corner of 23rd and Dodge Sts.

**Cost:** Free to visit during daylight hours with metered parking

**Pro Tip:** A Nebraska Historical marker for Capitol Hill is located on the grounds of Central High School.

# BENSON AND ITS BUNNIES

## How does a neighborhood grow?

In 1887, Omaha real estate speculator Erastus Benson purchased 900 acres of farmland located approximately nine miles northwest of Omaha on the Military Road. He soon platted a new community originally called Benson Place, began selling lots, and began building a streetcar line to connect his new town with Omaha. The Benson Motor Company started out using horse-drawn passenger cars until 1891, when the new Benson & Halcyon Heights Street Railway was organized to turn the line electric. At that time, there might have been 150 people in the little village. The new electric streetcars would run roughly two miles west and northwest from North 45th Street in the Walnut Hill neighborhood north and northwest along Military Avenue.

In 1899, Benson voters turned down a proposal to make the streetcar company a municipal publicly owned operation, and the next year it was purchased by the Omaha Street Railway. In 1915 town residents voted to build a new City Hall that still stands at 6008 Maple Street, and just two years later, Benson was annexed by the City of Omaha.

Like other real estate promoters of his time, Erastus Benson originally donated the land in his new town to build

## ERASTUS BENSON'S TOWN

**What:** A former town turned hip neighborhood

**Where:** The heart of Benson is along Maple St. between 60th and 63rd Sts.

**Cost:** Free

**Pro Tip:** See https:// waitingroomlounge.com/ to find out the new bands appearing at the The Waiting Room, the fabled live music venue in the old Lift Ticket Lounge

*The North 52nd Street entrance to Benson High School. Photograph courtesy of Michaela Armetta.*

a school. A new school building was constructed in 1904 at 5120 Maple Street. At some point in the 1920s, the school chose the somewhat unlikely name of the Bunnies for their mascot, although their athletic opponents learned not to laugh about it. A few more notable Benson students include football player Nile Kinnick, actor Nick Nolte, politician Hal Daub, and the authors Terry Goodkind and Robert Reed.

If you ask, everyone will claim they saw Nirvana play in Benson in 1989.

# ROSENFIELD'S PEONIES

## Where have all the flowers gone?

There was once a bright and vibrant novelty right along the Lincoln Highway on what were then the far western outskirts of Omaha. Transcontinental travelers would stop to gawk while local residents would head out across the farmlands just to see the 20 acres of peonies. This was the site of a nursery owned by John Rosenfield. He had started it on 10 acres in West Point, Nebraska, in the 1880s. During the early 1900s, Rosenfield introduced six new varieties of peonies, and in 1908 he brought out the Karl Rosenfield variety named after his son. Two years after that, he relocated his nursery business to 20 acres just west of Omaha, where he propagated his flowers for the next seven years. Rosenfield then sold the business and left Omaha, eventually retiring to Indianapolis, where he died in 1934.

All the people who went out to see the flowers also interested the three Malec brothers, Godfrey, Jerry, and Joe. In

## A PLACE FOR PEONIES

**What:** Site of a peony farm

**Where:** The site of Rosenfield's nursery was roughly between Cass St. and W. Dodge Rd. between N. 78th and N. 80th Sts.

**Cost:** Free to visit during daylight hours.

**Pro Tip:** The Karl Rosenfield peony remains one of the most popular varieties of the flower to this day.

Lawrence Welk's Orchestra was the house band at Peony Park's Terrace Ballroom during the 1930s.

*Looking west on West Dodge Road from 80th Street.*

1919, they opened a gas station that grew into an amusement park appropriately named Peony Park. A four-acre lake was added in the 1920s, with a ballroom and beer garden that made it a popular destination, at least for some. Peony Park was annexed into Omaha in 1958, but despite lawsuits, protests, and fines, it remained a segregated facility until 1963. Amusement rides were added in the 1970s, but Peony Park closed in 1994, and the site was redeveloped.

# THE BLOODY CORNER

## Who was that unidentified assassin?

As the "Magic City" of South Omaha boomed around the stockyards and slaughterhouses, it gained a reputation for booze and brawling that lingered long after it was annexed into Omaha. To this day, some Omahans proudly call themselves S.O.B.s. Still, even in South O, there was once a place that seemed even worse than the rest. It was the intersection of South 28th and R Streets that was once known as the "Bloody Corner" and had a distinct reputation for violence. That was back when there was a saloon on three of the corners joined by a low-end hotel on the fourth. The neighborhood around could be a rough and tumble mix of all sorts of people from everywhere. While passing through in 1889, English author Rudyard Kipling commented that Omaha "seemed to be populated entirely by Germans, Poles, Slavs, Hungarians, Croats, Magyars, and all the scum of Eastern Europe."

As for the "Bloody Corner," back in 1917, Omaha's *Bee* newspaper called the location a "notorious South Side spot . . . where many murders have occurred." Among the victims was Clinton Hartong, who was found dead on the sidewalk there one Saturday night in June 1922. According to the newspaper, the coroner's jury determined he'd "been killed by an unidentified assassin." The corner gradually lost it's infamous

*The Bloody Corner at South 28th and R Streets in 2020.*

identity. As of 2019, the Omaha Housing Authority planned to raze the neighborhood's Southside Terrace housing projects, the largest in Omaha, which were then home to 1,300 people.

The Southside Terrace housing projects on the west side of South 28th Street were built in the 1940s.

# OMAHA'S "PRETTIEST MILE"

## How can roads change a city?

There came a time in the late 19th century when civic leaders started to understand that sometimes a modern city needed more than just industrial smoke and squalor. In 1889 early American landscape architect H. W. S. Cleveland first proposed a system of boulevards and parkways to connect various public spaces. These new thoroughfares would be pleasantly decorated and well maintained. One of the Omaha's most historic was Florence Boulevard, which started in 1892 with improvements between Ames Avenue and Kansas Street and grew until it was called the city's "Prettiest Mile." The city's Park Department took over the project in 1897 as Florence Boulevard would run north from downtown up to the still-independent town of Florence and then into Miller Park. To this day, there remains an incredible variety of architectural styles all along the old boulevard. Today, the only original landscaping designs that remain are found between Fort and Read Streets.

Some of the more interesting houses include the one at 6327 Florence Boulevard, which was originally built at Fort Omaha in 1869 and moved to its present location around

**FLORENCE BOULEVARD**

**What:** Remnants of a 19th-century boulevard

**Where:** From 19th and Cass Sts. north to John J. Pershing Dr.

**Cost:** Free to travel during daylight hours

**Pro Tip:** A more modern Omaha boulevard is the Sorenson Parkway, which runs between Blair High Rd. and US Highway 75. It was constructed on the former route of the Fremont, Elkhorn & Missouri Valley Railroad.

*The former Broadview Hotel at 2060 Florence Boulevard was listed in
The Green Book.*

1900. At 6141 Florence is the only remaining house that Omaha's
one-time political boss Tom Dennison called home. There's also
the former Broadview Hotel at 2060 Florence. Otherwise known
as the Trimble Castle, this unique 1909 home was listed for many
years in the Green Book meant for Black travelers seeking safe
accommodations.

Tom Dennison moved out of his home on Florence
Boulevard shortly after the 1922 death of his first
wife Ada.

# PRESERVING SOME PRAIRIE

## What did Nebraska used to look like?

Less than two centuries ago, most of central North America was covered by dense grasslands that stretched on seemingly forever. In the tallgrass prairies, the grass would grow eight or more feet high, and fire only seemed to make it grow thicker.

To the west were the arid Great Plains, home to massive herds of buffalo and elk. The great wild herds are gone now, as are most of America's grasslands. The prairie was plowed under for farms as thousands of people took advantage of the Homestead Act to establish farms of their own.

Remnants of this former landscape are rare, but there have been an increasing number of attempts at restoring some of the land to a more natural state. Some dismiss the results of such efforts as just a weed-path instead of an incredibly diverse ecosystem. One of the earlier attempts to bring back some of the prairie originated in 1959, when Arthur and Antoinette Allwine donated their 160-acre farm to what was at the time the University of Omaha. The restoration of the prairie on the property began in 1970, and additional land was purchased in 2009 and 2013. The preserve now covers 525 acres and was renamed after the small spring-fed Glacier Creek.

Permanent environmental research facilities for the University of Nebraska's Biology Department are housed in a

*The barn at Glacier Creek Preserve. Photograph courtesy of Michaela Armetta.*

century-old barn that was moved to the site in 2012. There aren't any buffalo herds but there are over 350 different species of plants, an abundance of birds and insects, and a glimpse of what Nebraska used to look like.

The barn and silo were moved to the preserve from their original location at 180th and Ida Streets.

# A ROLLER COASTER DISASTER

## Why are roller coasters banned in Omaha?

It was a horrific accident at a place that had long advertised itself as Omaha's "Polite Resort." The place was originally established as Tietz Park in the mid-1880s by German immigrant Charles Tietz. It was located on the Military Road and hosted a concert every Sunday. There was a beer garden, dance hall, bowling alley, and likely a lot of German immigrants. After Tietz's death, ownership passed to Frederick Krug, Omaha's original Beer Baron. Krug was another German immigrant who moved to Omaha in 1858 and founded the city's first brewery the following year. It surely made sense for a beer brewer to own a summer resort that catered to German immigrants.

The different amusements at the renamed Krug Park grew to include a merry-go-round, picnic grounds, a swimming pool, an arcade, and the other expected summer amusements of the era. In 1918, the Big Dipper roller coaster opened, and while Prohibition shuttered the beer garden, the amusement park kept drawing crowds. In July 1930, four cars on the Big Dipper roller coaster left the tracks and fell 35 feet, trapping riders underneath and crushing others in the crowd. Four people were killed and 17 injured, and with that, the city council banned roller coasters from Omaha. There were dance marathons

You can see the last building left of the Fred Krug Brewing Company at 1207–1215 Jones Street

*The pool at Gallagher Park. Photo courtesy of Michaela Armetta.*

held there during the Great Depression, but perhaps it never seemed the same for some, as Krug Park closed in 1940.

Fifteen years later, the grounds became a more traditional city park that was later named for Rachel Gallagher, who had raised the funds to purchase the grounds.

## A PARK WITH A PAST

**What:** Site of an amusement park tragedy

**Where:** 2936 N. 56th St.

**Cost:** Free to visit during daylight hours.

**Pro Tip:** The name of the park lives on nearby at Krug Park: Beer, Bloody Marys & Spirits at 6205 Maple St.

# JOHN O'NEILL, THE HERO OF RIDGEWAY

## Who wouldn't invade Canada to free Ireland?

There's history and interesting views of Omaha around Holy Sepulchre Cemetery.

There's also one grave in particular that commemorates an American war hero of a different sort. This memorial was put up by Irish Nationalists in 1919 in commemoration of John O'Neill, the "Hero of Ridgeway," and was dedicated by Eamon De Valera, then the President of the Irish Republic. O'Neill had been born in County Monaghan, Ireland, in 1834 and emigrated across the Atlantic at the age of 14. He made his way out to California before serving in the Civil War. During the war, O'Neill joined the Fenians, a group of Irish Nationalists made up mostly of Union veterans determined to free Ireland from English domination by any means necessary.

Their curious plan for doing so seemed to be to seize Canada and demand Ireland's independence.

Thus, it was June 1866 when John O'Neill led a force of more than a thousand Fenians across the Niagara River into Canada. The Fenians overwhelmed the Canadian militia at the Battle of Ridgeway in the first armed effort for an independent Ireland in generations. Their victory was followed with a retreat back across the border before English reinforcements arrived. Four years later, O'Neill was less fortunate at the

*The grave of John O'Neill at Holy Sepulchre Cemetery.*

Battle of Eccles Hill near Frelighsburg, Quebec, and was arrested for violating America's neutrality laws. President Ulysses S. Grant pardoned him. After that, he got involved in Nebraska land speculation and encouraged Irish immigration around his namesake town of O'Neill, Nebraska. He died in 1878, and was buried in Omaha.

The remains of Thomas Cuming, the Acting Governor of Nebraska Territory who helped establish Omaha, were moved to Holy Sepulchre in the 1920s.

# A PAINTING ATTACKED TWICE

## How can art arouse such passions?

The painting's official title is *Le Printemps*, although it's better known as *The Return of Spring*. It was painted in 1886 by the French artist William-Adolphe Bouguereau and remains among his better-known works. The fate of many of his 822 known paintings remains a mystery. *The Return of Spring* features naked cherubs surrounding Bouguereau's envisioning of the nude figure of spring who barely covers her breasts while leaving everything else exposed.

The painting was first exhibited at the 1890 Omaha Art Exposition held at the building that still stands at 1221 Harney Street. *The Return of Spring* was for sale for $18,000, no small sum in those days. In December of that year, it was attacked with a chair by a young man named Carey Warbington, who told a local newspaper he only wanted to "protect the virtue of woman" and had never seen such a sight outside of a brothel. Well, who wanted to buy a damaged painting? The damaged painting, and the chair, were moved to the New York Life Insurance Building

George Lininger paid for sculptor Gutzon Borglum to study in Europe years before he carved Mt. Rushmore.

*The Joslyn Art Museum on Dodge Street.*

at 1650 Farnam Street and put on display for a quarter admission. In the end, a former implement dealer turned art collector named George Lininger did buy it. It was gifted to the Joslyn Art Museum in 1951 and was attacked again in 1976. Again, someone took exception to the shameless nudity and sensuality. The painting has been restored and is now kept under glass.

# WHO KILLED HARRY LAPIDUS?

## What was the price on his head?

Tom Dennison's hold over Omaha was almost at its end by December 1931 when his corrupt political machine killed Harry Lapidus. Sure, the gangsters who'd dominated Omaha's politics and vice for decades had already orchestrated a downtown lynching and killed a few bootleggers, but Harry Lapidus was something else. He was the President of the Omaha Fixture and Supply Company, he had national connections, and he was well known for his charity. He was also the father-in-law of Nebraska's Assistant Attorney General. Two nights before Christmas Eve, Lapidus left the Jewish Community Center in his LaSalle sedan. A nearby resident reported it was north of the intersection of 19th Street and Park Avenue across from the lagoon where another automobile pulled alongside. Two men got out, and there were words. Then someone shot Harry Lapidus three times in the head. The men then got back into their car and left.

The police had 10 men and one woman in custody by Christmas Day, but they were all soon released. Rumors and even manufactured evidence insinuated that Lapidus was as dirty as the rest and that his own involvement in bootlegging was what got him killed. Dennison allies on the police force were put in charge, and no one bothered to preserve the crime scene.

## MURDER BY A PARK

**What:** Site of an unsolved gangland murder

**Where:** S. 19th St. across from the Hanscom Park lagoon

**Cost:** Free to visit during daylight hours

**Pro Tip:** The Gerald R. Ford Birthsite and Gardens are located nearby at 3202 Woolworth Ave.

*The lagoon at Hanscom Park looking towards South 19th Street.*

There was talk of a bungled kidnapping. It was also said Dennison had offered $1,000 to kill Lapidus. It would never be proved, but everyone knew. At the next election, Dennison's political machine was replaced even as a federal liquor indictment revealed there really was no Prohibition in Omaha as long as you were willing to pay. Dennison relocated to California, and died in 1934.

Hanscom is Omaha's oldest city park and was donated in 1872.

# BEADLE'S ROCK BROOK CLAIM

## What was it like when the West was still wild?

In 1857 a New Yorker named Erastus Beadle headed out west to make his mark in Nebraska Territory. Like so many others, he was going to try and get rich by promoting real estate in a brand-new speculative town. Bare dirt one week could be worth $50 as a platted city lot a week later, $500 the week after that, and then sometimes $6 six months later. All sorts of new places popped up in the 1850s along the west bank of the Missouri River. One of them was called Saratoga and went bust within a year. Beadle then moved farther west on the prairies and bought a claim from a man called Dick Darling. Darling claimed to be among the earliest settlers in the region around Omaha, where he'd lived in a log cabin shack for three years.

The claim Beadle was interested in was located mostly along the west bank of the Big Papillion. According to his journal, there was "a small grove, a number of springs, and a stone quarry" and otherwise "as far as the eye could see was a wide expanse of rolling prairie, unmolested by the hand of Man." The claim included another, smaller stream that was the first Beadle ever saw "in the west with stone bottom." He called his new home Rock Brook Farm. At the end of 1857, he returned east, where he embarked on a long career as part of Beadle

Towl Park is an access point for the Big Papio Trail.

*The Big Papillion Creek looking north.*

and Adams, publishers. The first Beadle's dime novel came out in 1860 and would be followed by 629 more. The view from Beadle's farm is a bit different today, but it does include the Happy Hollow country club, Rock Brook shopping plaza at 2800 South 110th Court, and Towl Park at 9310 West Center Road.

**What:** Site of the Nebraska Territory land claim of a dime novel publisher

**Where:** Beadle's original claim was north of W. Center Rd., west of the Big Papillion, south of Woolworth Ave., and east of 105th St.

**Cost:** Free to view during daylight hours.

**Pro Tip:** The Beadle & Adams dime novel *California Joe, the Mysterious Plainsman* can be seen at web.stanford.edu/dept/SUL/library/prod/depts/dp/pennies/texts/ingraham2_toc.html

# MINNE LUSA

## How does architecture define a place?

It was Omaha's largest development of the time with a soothing name of indeterminate origin. Perhaps Minne Lusa came from the Native American name for a nearby stream, or else might have been a corruption of the name of Spanish-born explorer Manuel Lisa. Either way, the Minne Lusa neighborhood had its start in 1916, when Charles Martin bought a 128-acre cornfield north of Miller Park. It took seven years for Martin to develop the land into 800 lots on the 33 blocks of his new neighborhood. Most lots sold from $450 to $1000, and Martin bragged that there were 12 miles of sidewalks and 1,700 shade trees. The majority of homes are Craftsman bungalows, with several larger homes fronting the serpentine Minne Lusa Boulevard, which runs down the middle of the development. Martin made money out of Minne Lusa so fast that he bought more land to the north and west to establish the Florence Field development.

Many homes were altered over the years but there remain 540 properties in Minne Lusa that contributed to its historic

The Minne Lusa neighborhood was listed on the National Register of Historic Places in 2014.

*Some Minne Lusa bungalows and the World War I monument.*

designation. Many of them were designed by Omaha architect Everett S. Dodds. In 1914 Dodds published a catalog of Craftsman designs which can still be seen in Minne Lusa and around the region. Some of the notable homes can be seen right along Minne Lusa Boulevard, including Charles Martin's own Mission-style home at 6078 Minne Lusa Boulevard. Bungalow-lovers of all sorts should take a drive through the side streets as well and maybe find a place to stay forever. A World War I monument placed by the Omaha Chapter of American War Mothers sits at the southern entrance of Minne Lusa Boulevard directly across from Miller Park.

# SOME COPENHAGEN IN OMAHA

## Where can you find dragon tails in Omaha?

There'd been Danish immigrants around Omaha since the city's earliest days, although it's a long way from the sea. By 1890, there were more Danes in Iowa and Nebraska than anywhere else in the country. It was in Omaha in 1872 where the Danish language newspaper *Den Danske Pioneer* had its start. The Pioneer became the source for all Danes in America. It moved to suburban Chicago in 1958 and still exists as part of Bertelsen Publishing.

Another reminder of Omaha's rich Danish roots in the city was the 1881 organization of the Danish Arms Brothers. These were Danish immigrant veterans who'd fought either in the Civil War or in the wars with Prussia over Schleswig-Holstein. Other branches soon appeared in neighboring states. In January 1882, they held a convention in Omaha to organize the Danish Brotherhood of America, a fraternal organization that was meant to continue their heritage and traditions and also to provide insurance benefits for members.

In 1966, the Danish Brotherhood in America built a new Omaha headquarters with an unusual flair. Omaha architect Edward Sessinghaus was chosen for the project and incorporated a variety of distinctly Scandinavian elements into

### DANISH INSURANCE

**What:** Former headquarters of an insurance company with a Danish past

**Where:** 3717 Harney St.

**Cost:** Free to view during daylight hours with metered parking

**Pro Tip:** Omaha's Danish American Society has a hall available for rent at 9100 N. 31st St.

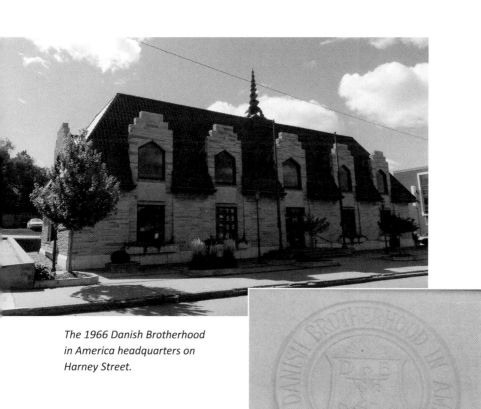

The 1966 Danish Brotherhood
in America headquarters on
Harney Street.

the building's design, including the roof and second-story windows
and especially that spire. That was something rather rare in a 1960s
building and was patterned after the entwined dragon-tail tower
atop Copenhagen's old stock exchange, *Børsbygningen*. The Danish
Brotherhood merged into the Woodmen of the World in 2016, but
the dragon tails remain.

The Danish Brotherhood headquarters was listed
on the National Register of Historic Places in 2016.

# THE ELMWOOD GROTTO

## Where did you go get your water?

Omaha's city parks cover 11,000 acres, but one of the more interesting will always be Elmwood. The park was first established in 1890 on what was then the city's western outskirts and was expanded to over 200 acres within the first three years. In 1896, some 3,000 people went to the park to celebrate the 4th of July. In 1909, a pavilion was added that's still available for rent. There's also a public swimming pool and an 18-hole golf course. For decades, a Swedish folk festival was held annually in the park, which remains a popular place for reunions, picnics, and students from nearby University of Nebraska at Omaha. Over the years, Elmwood has also provided convenient parking for student vehicles, and in 1970, a parking garage for students was planned for a portion of the park. Public outcry led by parks advocate Rachel Gallagher eventually scuttled the proposal.

## FORGOTTEN SPRINGS

**What:** A scenic grotto

**Where:** 809 S. 60th St.

**Cost:** Free to visit during daylight hours

**Pro Tip:** Shakespeare on the Green is held annually at Elmwood so that plays can be performed as they were meant to be seen. Please see https://www.nebraskashakespeare.com/shakespeare-on-the-green.

One of the more secretive and unique areas of Elmwood is its shaded grotto near the banks of Elmwood Creek. For many years, the natural springs that flowed out of the ground provided fresh water for drinking and washing, and hundreds went there daily. A trough for the convenience of the public was eventually constructed and remains there today, although the water was shut off for sanitary reasons long ago. The springs now merely help keep Elmwood creek flowing southwest into

*The water trough at the Elmwood Park grotto.*

the Little Papillion Creek adjacent to the Keystone Trail. Regardless of the season, the grotto seems tucked away from the rest of the city as a shaded bit of seclusion often used for weddings and photographs.

The 1927 pedestal erected by the Omaha Amateur Baseball Association lost its statue to a WWII metal drive.

# THE MURDER AT THE UNIVERSITY OF OMAHA

## Who killed Carolyn Nevins?

There was a tragedy in Omaha in December 1955, the month Rosa Parks refused to give up her seat on a Montgomery, Alabama, bus. That tragedy soon turned into a mystery. Over time, the murder of Carolyn Nevins became folklore and finally legend. It remains an unsolved murder that took place right outside the first building constructed on the campus of what used to be the University of Omaha.

In other places, the Georgian Revival college building might be dubbed Old Main. Instead, the present day Arts and Sciences Hall was built in 1938 after the university left its old campus behind. The college had its start in 1908 in the Kountze Place neighborhood with the first classes held in the Redick Mansion—which was moved in 1917 to a Minnesota lake resort, where it burned down in 1938. None of the buildings of the original campus remain.

"Sixteen Tons" was the radio hit in December 1955 when 20-year-old Carolyn Nevins was shot to death while waiting on a ride. It was said she was still holding her bus fare in her hand. Ms. Nevins was a senior majoring in sociology and speech and was considered a bright and cheerful presence on campus. It all happened some time after she left the university's library at 11:00 at night. She was shot four times with a .32 pistol and left to die as the temperature dropped down to 17 degrees. There were few clues. It all seemed so sudden and so random,

---

The University of Omaha became a part of the University of Nebraska system in 1968.

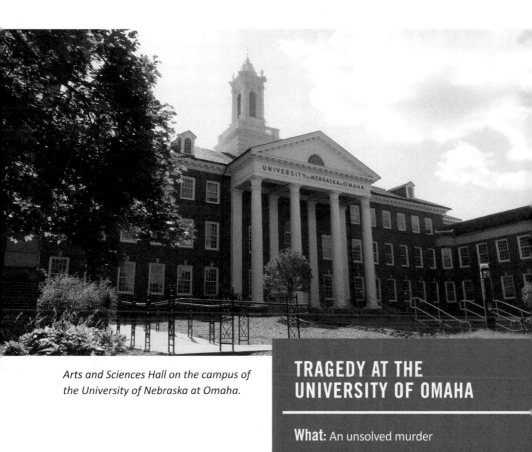

*Arts and Sciences Hall on the campus of the University of Nebraska at Omaha.*

## TRAGEDY AT THE UNIVERSITY OF OMAHA

**What:** An unsolved murder

**Where:** Arts and Sciences Hall is at 222 University Dr.

**Cost:** Free to visit during daylight hours

**Pro Tip:** There's more to see, and a map of the University's Dodge St. campus can be found at www.unomaha.edu/about-uno/buildings-and-maps/_assets/img/dodge-campus-map.pdf

with only a "tall, dark, slender man" reported near Ms. Nevins at the bus stop 300 feet from Arts and Sciences Hall. The police gave 92 lie detector tests during the first six months of the investigation but got nowhere. There was an October 1956 confession from a California man that turned into nothing. The last time the police had a look seemed to be a bullet comparison in 1982. The murder of Carolyn Nevins remains unsolved.

# SHEELYTOWN

## What's worth burning down a church?

The Irish may have started out there, but in Omaha Sheelytown and Polish became synonymous long ago. The neighborhood was named after the Sheely Brothers and their packinghouse, which operated during the 1880s near Martha and South 27th Streets. By 1884, Sheely was the third-largest packer in Omaha. The massive nearby Union Stockyards made it convenient for newly arrived immigrants looking for work, and the proximity of the odoriferous packinghouse provided a reason for others to stay away. The Sheely Brothers packinghouse burned to the ground in 1886, but the name of the neighborhood stuck. In addition to the Polish, Czech and German immigrants also moved in, and the area became part of Omaha in 1887.

Neighborhood borders can be fluid, but Sheelytown generally encompassed everything between Hanscom Park and the Union Stock Yards.

It was a working class, ethnic neighborhood where few spoke English. It was best known for its extravagant weddings and its dances and polka bands. In 1895, the Sheelytown church war broke out over control of St. Paul's Catholic Church, which stood at Elm and South 29th Streets.

The Bishop of Omaha was on one side, and a faction led by Polish nationalist Stanislaus Kaminski was on the other. There was a shootout, and in the end, someone burned the

## A HISTORIC POLISH NEIGHBORHOOD

**What:** Site of a historic neighborhood

**Where:** Vinton St. north to Edward Creighton Blvd. between S. 24th and S. 34th Sts.

**Cost:** Free to visit during daylight hours

**Pro Tip:** Check out Frank Stoysich Meats at 5170 Q St. ( https://www.frankstoysichmeats.com) for something special.

*Dinker's Bar and the mural for Sheelytown.*

church down. Kaminski's faction was officially blamed. Sheelytown even had its own unofficial mayor, saloon owner Nicodemus Dargaczewski, back during the days when Tom Dennison was in control. By 1940 there were almost 14,000 Polish immigrants and their descendants in Douglas County, with many still living in the old neighborhood. In the 1960s, construction of Interstate 480 buried much of Sheelytown under concrete, and today there are only a handful of remnants left of what was once a different sort of place.

The Polish commemorative mural is at Dinker's Bar at 2368 South 29th Street.

# WALK WITH STANDING BEAR

## How far can you walk?

There's a 135-acre lake out in Omaha's western suburbs that started out simply as Dam Site 16. It was created as one of several efforts meant to control flooding along Papillion Creek and its tributaries. One of the worst floods followed eight inches of rain in two days in June 1964. Seven people died as thousands of acres were flooded. Normally torpid Hell Creek turned into a torrent, with five-foot waves crashing down the tributary of the Papillion's West Branch to knock homes off foundations. In Millard, 95 trailers were carried away. Standing Bear Lake opened to the public in 1977 as a new area for recreation and to help control the flooding. In 2020, a 975-foot-long "floating trail" was constructed for those who want to walk on the waters.

The park was named after Standing Bear, the Ponca Chief who changed American history. Like so many others, the Ponca were forced to leave their homes and relocate to Indian Territory, where times proved more than hard. In 1878 Standing Bear's son Bear Shield died. Standing Bear set out to return his son's remains to their home along the Niobrara River. A small group joined him, but instead of finding peace, Standing Bear and his small band of Ponca were arrested by federal authorities while they were guests on the Omaha Reservation. Standing Bear and the others were taken to the City of Omaha, where he

There are 396 acres around Standing Bear Lake, which is about 24 feet deep.

*The floating trail at Standing Bear Lake. Photograph courtesy of Michaela Armetta.*

sued for habeas corpus in the United States District Court. His case was the first in which American law recognized that a Native American was legally a person. Standing Bear died in 1908 in his home along the Niobrara River, where the Ponca Tribe of Nebraska still lives today.

## WATER WALKWAY AT STANDING BEAR LAKE

**What:** Walk on the water

**Where:** 6404 N. 132nd St.

**Cost:** Free to visit during daylight hours

**Pro Tip:** There's a Nebraska historical marker about Standing Bear near the boat ramp north of Fort and N. 138th Sts.

# THAT FLORENCE BANK

## What happens when money just becomes pretty paper?

What is likely Omaha's oldest building sits somewhat quietly on the west side of North 30th Street in what used to be the independent town of Florence. This was one of Nebraska Territory's original communities, established in 1854 by James Mitchell around the site of the old Mormon Winter Quarters. Florence may be older, but it was Omaha City just downriver that would win the coveted position as territorial capital. In early 1858, an illegal session of Nebraska's territorial legislature was held in Florence to escape Omaha City's odious and omnipresent influence. Bellevue's *Gazette* newspaper praised this as "required by honor and [the] true interest of the Territory" and congratulated all those legislators "outside of Omaha" who met in Florence. The *Gazette* made sure to reprint an item snipped from the *Hawk-Eye* newspaper of Burlington, Iowa, concerning the "scheme of corruption" at Omaha City "for the benefit of Eastern politicians." The Florence legislature proclaimed Thomas Cuming an "accidental Executive" and voted for many things, including incorporating the towns of Beatrice and Tecumseh, approving the divorce of Jason and Salvina Hickman, and amending the charter of the Bank of Florence.

The Bank of Florence was founded in 1856 as one of the "wildcat" banks that printed their own currency, backed only by speculation, hope, and inflation instead of gold or anything

The three-dollar bill issued by the Bank of Florence featured an unknown woman, a rustic farm scene, and chickens.

*The Bank of Florence and historical marker on North 30th Street.*

else. The Panic of 1857 crashed the local economy as the Bank of Florence and all of Nebraska Territory's wildcat banks closed. Investors lost everything, as all those pretty bank notes proved to be worth nothing. The old bank has been part of Omaha ever since Florence was annexed in 1917.

## THE 1856 BANK OF FLORENCE BUILDING

**What:** Omaha's oldest building

**Where:** 8502 N. 30th St.

**Cost:** For hours and admission, please contact the Florence Historical Foundation at 402-453-4280.

**Pro Tip:** Another of Nebraska Territory's wildcat banks that is still standing is the Fontenelle Bank located at 2212 Main St. in Bellevue.

# UNION PACIFIC SHOP YARDS MONUMENT

## Where did you work on the railroad?

It became a tangle of tracks and cinders where the Hell on Wheels had its real start. That conglomeration of gamblers, prostitutes, and ne'er-do-wells all kicked off in Omaha when the Union Pacific Railroad started building west to complete the transcontinental railroad. When Abraham Lincoln signed the Pacific Railway Act into law in 1862, Omaha's future seemed forever secure as one of the country's major points of transit. The groundbreaking of the Union Pacific was held the next year near Davenport and North 7th Streets, and the nearby shop yards would play an important role in the development of Omaha and the West. It was there, north of downtown Omaha, that some of the first rails were laid to eventually meet with the Central Pacific in 1869 to connect the continent.

Today, there is a small memorial and even green grass to commemorate a place that was dominated by grit, noise, and hard work not so long ago. The Union Pacific's Omaha shop yards would grow with the railroad and the country through the years. The end came in 1988, when the Union Pacific moved its maintenance facility to Arkansas. The neighborhood was

---

### THE UP SHOPS

**What:** Monument for a former railroad yard

**Where:** Southwest corner of the intersection of N. 10th and Cuming Sts.

**Cost:** Free to visit during daylight hours

**Pro Tip:** The dining facility at the current Union Pacific Railroad headquarters at 1400 Douglas St. is open to the public. Please contact the Union Pacific at 402-544-5000 for specific hours.

*The monument to the Union Pacific Railroad's Omaha shop yards at North 10th and Cuming Streets.*

drastically transformed with construction of the current CHI Health Center at 455 North 10th Street in 2003 and the TD Ameritrade ballpark at 1200 Mike Fahey Street in 2011. The stadium was meant to be the new home for the NCAA College World Series of Baseball, an event held annually in Omaha since 1950.

There were 152 streamlined, internal combustion McKeen Motor Cars manufactured at Omaha's Union Pacific shop yards between 1905 and 1917.

# GOOSE HOLLOW

## Where did all the workers live?

Omaha's Happy Hollow neighborhood west of Dundee is well-known for its shaded streets and stately Tudor Revival homes, but Goose Hollow is a different sort of place. This was a neighborhood of closely packed cottages tucked down in a dale with enormous packinghouses all around. Goose Hollow was named after its flocks of backyard fowl and became the center of the city's Croatian and Slovenian immigrant community. The packinghouses offered these immigrants the promise of steady but sometimes dangerous and often grotesque work. By 1910, livestock traded annually included 1.2 million cattle and 1.9 million hogs with most making their way to the nearby South Omaha packinghouses.

In 1907 a group of Croatian immigrants first gathered in the home of Nicholas Mickells to attend church services given by Father John Zaplotnik. Zaplotnik was born in the foothills of the Alps at Kranjska Gora, Slovenia, and immigrated to the United States as a child. He came to South Omaha after he was ordained in 1908 to serve the city's growing immigrant population, which at the time numbered around 175 families. Ten years later, in August 1917, a parade was held to lay the cornerstone of what the *Bee* newspaper proclaimed the "only Croatian church in Nebraska," which became Saints Peter

## A HISTORIC CROATIAN NEIGHBORHOOD

**What:** A historic ethnic neighborhood

**Where:** Along V and W Sts. from S. 31 west to S. 34th St.

**Cost:** Free to visit during daylight hours

**Pro Tip:** Saints Peter and Paul Catholic Church at 5912 S. 36th St. is home to the annual Greatest Festival in Town. Visit https://stspeterpaulomaha.org/festival/ for more information.

*The Croatian mural at Bere's Hall.*

and Paul Catholic Church. There Father Zaplotnik gave services alternately in Croatian, Slovenian, and English and reportedly had to deal with the occasional agitator who would stand in the back and call out "Pope laz!" or "The Pope lies." A parochial school was started adjacent in 1926, and the current Saints Peter and Paul church was dedicated in 1967 with a definite Modernist appeal.

The *Zajednica* mural in honor of the Croatian community was dedicated in 2017 on the south side of Bere's Hall at 3616 W Street.

# CUT-OFF ISLAND

## What state are you in?

Everyone knows that Nebraska is west of the Missouri River. Everyone also knows that Iowa is on the east side of the Big Muddy. And yet, it's still possible to easily pass back and forth between the two without getting your feet wet and, for many, without even noticing. That's because Carter Lake, Iowa, is surrounded by Omaha, Nebraska, excepting one small sliver along the Missouri River. It is a place long known for legal contests over taxation and legal jurisdiction. Sometimes it seemed those in Omaha wanted to take it over and sometimes it seemed they wished it would just go away.

In 1877 the Missouri River decided to relocate into a new channel and left behind what came to be called Cut-Off Island. No one cared much what went on there. Only after some land promoters got the idea to establish an industrial suburb called East Omaha there did people start to pay attention. Factories opened, and cottages were built for workers along with a streetcar line that ran on

### SMALL TOWN IN A BIG CITY

**What:** A small Iowa town surrounded by Omaha

**Where:** Carter Lake is easily accessed via Abbott St. or Locust St.

**Cost:** Free to visit during daylight hours

**Pro Tip:** Council Bluffs, Nebraska, and Iowa all sued to stop it, but in 2019 the Ponca Tribe of Nebraska opened their Prairie Flower Casino at 1031 Ave. H East in Carter Lake.

During the 1940s, Carter Lake's Chez Paree nightclub was dubbed the most notorious gambling spot between Chicago and Reno.

*The border of Iowa and Nebraska looking west on Avenue H.*

Locust Street west to North 16th Street in Omaha. The issue over whether the land was in Iowa or Nebraska went all the way to the United States Supreme Court in 1892. The court ruled that some of East Omaha was really still in Iowa. After that, the area was legally part of Council Bluffs for taxation purposes but still lacked paved streets and sewers. In the 1920s, residents revolted and voted to secede from Council Bluffs and instead formed their own unique municipality as a bit of Iowa west of the river.

# HUMMEL PARK

## How many steps are there?

In the hills up in the northern parts of Omaha, there's a public park whose rich historical significance has often been overshadowed by folklore. This is Hummel Park, named after the genial German immigrant Joseph Hummel. As a longtime Omaha city councilman, Hummel served as overseer of Omaha's park system as well as a reliable friend of Tom Dennison. The 202-acre tract was given to the city in 1930, and rumors have long circulated (without any actual evidence) of lynchings and satanic sacrifice. There are hiking trails through the woods with a Devil's Slide down the eroding cliffs, a historic picnic pavilion, and stone steps that seem to change in number depending on who's counting them.

There's also a small historical marker at the northern entrance to Hummel Park that commemorates two once-significant sites that have been mostly forgotten. Somewhere nearby, no one is really sure, was the site of Fort Lisa, which was established sometime between 1807 and 1812 by the famed fur trader Manuel Lisa for his Missouri Fur Company. It was the fur trade that first brought the Native Americans who lived along the Missouri River into a larger economic system that stretched to Europe in an era when men wore beaver felt

## A HISTORIC PARK

**What:** A public park with history and legends.

**Where:** The historical marker is at John J. Pershing Dr. and Hummel Rd.

**Cost:** Free to visit during daylight hours.

**Pro Tip:** Follow the road north from Hummel Park and eventually find your way to the original Council Bluffs where Lewis and Clark first met with the Otoe and Missouria. This is now Fort Atkinson State Historical Park at 201 S. 7th St. in Fort Calhoun, Nebraska.

*The lodge and monument to Fort Lisa and Jean Pierre Cabanne at Hummel Park.*

hats. During its heyday, Fort Lisa was the major center of growing American influence in the region and destination for the steamboat *Western Engineer*, the first steamboat to travel that far up the Missouri River in 1819. The marker also noted the location, some 385 feet southeast, as the site of the trading post run by Jean Pierre Cabanne. This was for the American Fur Company of St. Louis, which came to dominate the fur trade throughout the West. Cabanne's Post was closed sometime in the early 1830s and was relocated south to what is now Bellevue.

Those who spread rumors of an albino colony at Hummel Park had more likely spotted some of the nudists who organized nearby in 1934.

# A GERMAN PRINCE AND GEORGE WASHINGTON

## How many types of flowers can you find?

There are plenty of scenic views in the hills of eastern Omaha, but there's only one that includes a half-sized replica of George Washington's garden at Mt. Vernon. Washington designed his own gardens overlooking the Potomac River, but Omaha's version was scaled down by landscape architect George Hood. Mt. Vernon Gardens covers just over 31 acres and was opened in 1931. In the years since, the park has provided a site for many pleasing picnics and has long been a popular place for weddings. In spring and summer, the many varieties of flowers and lush greenery make for a pleasant stroll. In winter, the lack of leaves on the trees only improves the sometimes snowy view overlooking the Missouri River valley.

There is also a small monument at Mt. Vernon Gardens that is dedicated to Prince Maximilian of Wied-Neuwied. The Prince was an explorer of some repute as well as a naturalist and ethnologist who served in the Prussian Army during the Napoleonic Wars. From 1817 to 1819, Prince Maximilian explored southeastern Brazil and wrote an early account of its people and environment. In 1833 and 1834, he was accompanied by the Swiss artist Karl Bodmer on his exploration of the Missouri River as far north and west as present-day Montana. The account of his North American adventures was published between 1839 and 1841, and Prince Maximilian

Many of Karl Bodmer's paintings of the 1833–34 exploration are on display at the Joslyn Art Museum at 2200 Dodge Street.

*Prince Maximilian's marker at Mt. Vernon Gardens.*

continued to write about what he found until his 1867 death. Items he collected on his travels are still on display at a museum in Stuttgart, Germany, while the now bullet-scarred marker in Omaha was erected by the city's German immigrant residents in 1934.

## MT. VERNON GARDENS IN OMAHA

**What:** George Washington's garden in miniature, with a marker for a German prince

**Where:** 6011 S. 13th St.

**Cost:** Free to visit during daylight hours

**Pro Tip:** Adjoining is Mandan Park at 6215 S. 13th St. that offers additional scenic views along with informational panels about Lewis and Clark's travels through the area in the early 1800s.

# THE ORIGINAL OMAHA

## Who lived here before?

No, we'll never really know what its original inhabitants used to call this place that became Omaha, Nebraska. Still, in the 18th century—and likely earlier—a Native American village stood on the site of the current city. Were these people Omaha or Pawnee? Were they Ioway, Otoe, Ponca, or even another tribe before that?

The official record varies, and we'll never really know the history of all the earlier residents of the present city. Development in the years since has long since disturbed and reburied most of the archaeological sites that may have existed. In 1797, the location was already noted to be abandoned when Scottish-born adventurer and fur trader James MacKay passed by on his way up the Missouri River. Mackay called this place the "old village" of Iowa and Otoe. That settlement might have dated from the days when those inhabitants adapted to the local lifestyle of planting corn and hunting buffalo, or maybe it didn't.

Seven years after MacKay, the American explorers Lewis and Clark ventured up the Missouri River and also commented on what they supposed to be an old Otoe village. By that time, all that remained were mounds of dirt, the remnants of the earth lodges the people of this area built as homes.

According to early Omaha historian Alfred Sorenson, this early Native American town was much larger than one might presume and was spread across some 200 acres. There's a

The archway at Farnam and South 11th Street formerly graced the Corey-McKenzie Building located at Farnam and South 12th Streets.

*Looking north from South 11th and Farnam Streets.*

Nebraska historical marker about the location located on the Creighton University campus at 1821 California Street.

## A PLACE BEFORE OMAHA

**What:** Site of a historic Native American settlement

**Where:** North and east of 11th and Farnam Sts.

**Cost:** Free to visit during daylight hours with metered parking

**Pro Tip:** *Heritage*, designed by Nebraska sculptor Herb Mignery, portrays a pioneer American family and was dedicated in 1984 on Douglas St. just east of S. 13th St.

# ONLY GOVERNOR FOR TWO DAYS

## What if Francis Burt had lived?

Everything around Omaha would surely have been very different if only Francis Burt hadn't gotten so sick. In 1854 President Franklin Pierce appointed the ambitious South Carolina politician as the first governor of the new Nebraska Territory. Burt was from Pendleton, South Carolina, where he got into politics in 1832 as one of the Nullificationists who wanted to 'nullify' federal laws regarding tariffs and slavery. Burt went on to be elected to the South Carolina state legislature, served a term as State Treasurer, and was a member of the 1852 South Carolina Constitutional Convention.

His 1854 appointment in Nebraska seemed just another step in a long political career. He set out with one of his sons and a few neighbors in early September. On his way to his new home, Burt grew ill and was in sorry shape when his party finally reached Bellevue on October 6. Bellevue was the only real semblance of American settlement in the new territory, and Burt found refuge at the Presbyterian Mission House. This was a sprawling log structure constructed in 1846 as a place to convert Nebraska's Native Americans to what the settlers considered a more civilized religion and way of life. A grand reception was held in honor of Burt's arrival, but he was too ill even to attend, and the speeches promoting Nebraska's glorious future went

---

When Thomas Cuming was serving as Acting Governor of Nebraska Territory, he and his wife actually lived at the Pacific House Hotel in Council Bluffs, Iowa.

The Bellevue marker commemorating the Bellevue Presbyterian Mission.

on without him. On October 16, Burt was given the oath of office to oversee and shape the new American territory. Two days later, Francis Burt died at the mission. His successor was Acting Governor Thomas Cuming, who fell in league with the Council Bluffs ferry company to promote a place called Omaha City instead of the older and more obvious Bellevue. Their schemes succeeded as Omaha was named the first capital of the territory and grew to become Nebraska's metropolis along the Missouri River.

## THE PRESBYTERIAN MISSION

**What:** Marker commemorating the Bellevue Presbyterian Mission

**Where:** 1907 Warren St.

**Cost:** Free to view during daylight hours

**Pro Tip:** In spite of a somewhat sketchy history, the log cabin at nearby 1805 Hancock Street is said to be Nebraska's oldest building and was moved to its current location in 1850.

# THE GOLDEN SPIKE

## Why is America's largest golden spike in Council Bluffs?

On May 10, 1869, Leland Stanford drove the famed golden spike at Promontory Summit, Utah, to mark the completion of the transcontinental railroad. The Pacific Ocean was connected to the Atlantic across the United States just ten years after Abraham Lincoln had visited Council Bluffs.

There were really four different spikes used, including a silver spike from the State of Nevada and a hybrid iron, silver, and gold one from Arizona Territory. They were tapped in gently, so as not to damage their value. The ceremonial spikes were then promptly pulled back out and replaced by ordinary iron spikes. The original Golden Spike is at the Cantor Arts Center at Stanford University in California.

Seventy years after that historic event movie director Cecil B. DeMille's glorified motion picture extravaganza *Union Pacific* premiered at the Paramount, Orpheum, and the Omaha theaters downtown. The movie was based on a 1936 novel by Ernest Haycox and starred Joel McRea and Barbara Stanwyck in a heavily fictionalized account of construction of the railroad westward across the continent. It was a major event, as Hollywood movies rarely premiered in Omaha. Omaha's men grew beards, and downtown was dudded up with old-time false fronts to commemorate an

### A GIANT GOLDEN SPIKE

**What:** A 56-foot-tall concrete replica of a railroad spike painted gold

**Where:** Ninth Ave. and S. 21st St. in Council Bluffs

**Cost:** Free to visit during daylight hours

**Pro Tip:** The nearby tavern The O Face at 2400 Ninth Ave. won some measure of infamy when it was featured on the television show *Bar Rescue*.

*The Golden Spike Monument on 9th Avenue in Council Bluffs, Iowa.*

earlier era of the city. There was a grand parade and May bonnets. During these celebrations, the City of Council Bluffs constructed a 56-foot-tall concrete replica of the famed Golden Spike. President of the Union Pacific William Jeffers dedicated the new monument at what was legally considered the eastern terminus of the transcontinental route.

Council Bluffs is home to the Union Pacific Railroad Museum at 200 Pearl Street.

# THE GENERAL IN A GARDEN

## How did an Old West Army General live?

He was known as one of America's greatest Indian fighters and one of the best friends the Native Americans had. George Crook came from Ohio and graduated near the bottom of his class at West Point in 1852. He was sent to California and the Pacific Northwest to fight Native Americans. At the outbreak of the Civil War, Crook became a Colonel of the 36th Ohio Infantry and he rose through the ranks before and after his success at the Battle of Antietam. He was given command over the Department of Western Virginia in 1864 during the campaign through the Shenandoah Valley. Crook was also captured in early 1865 in Maryland and was held briefly in the Confederate capital Richmond. After the Civil War ended, Crook was sent back to the Pacific Northwest and the "Snake War" against the Northern Paiute. He was then sent to Arizona to force the Yavapai and Tonto Apache onto the land where the government wanted them.

Crook's appointment as head of the US Army's Department of the Platte from 1875 to 1882 and from 1886 to 1888 brought him to Omaha. These were the years of the Plains Indian

### STATUE OF GENERAL GEORGE CROOK

**What:** Statue of a famous American General

**Where:** In the garden of the General George Crook House at 5730 N. 30th St., #11B

**Cost:** Normal cost of the museum may apply.

**Pro Tip:** Fort Omaha is now Metropolitan Community College but retains an interesting and stately atmosphere. A worthwhile tour can be found at https://northomahahistory.com/noh-guide-to-fort-omaha-4/

*General George Crook at the historic Fort Omaha.*

wars against the Cheyenne and Lakota. Crook led the so-called "Horsemeat March" of 1876 in pursuit of those responsible for Little Big Horn, and on that march, soldiers were forced to eat their mounts in the Dakota Badlands. In 1879, General Crook had the Commander's Home built at Fort Omaha, and that same year, he arrested the Ponca Chief Standing Bear in a landmark legal case described on pages 58–59. Crook then returned to Arizona Territory and forced the surrender of the Apache leader Geronimo. Having seen too many broken treaties, General Crook later worked to better the treatment of Native Americans by the government. He died in 1890 in Chicago.

Fort Crook in nearby Bellevue was named after the General and is now Offutt Air Force Base.

# SITE OF COURTLAND BEACH

## Want to go for a swim?

There was once an amusement park dubbed Courtland Beach along the south shore of what used to be the Saratoga Bend of the Missouri River. After 1877, most people called it Cut-Off Lake before it became Carter Lake. Levi Carter owned the lead works at East Omaha, and it was his widow who'd donated the land on the lake's north shore that gave the oxbow its long-accepted name. It was Courtland Beach that would make the lake a place for bathing, amusements, and more.

The amusement park at Courtland Beach opened in 1889, before the question over East Omaha's legal status was settled (see pages 66–67). It started as a typical lakeside summer resort with boating, bathing, live music, and relaxation. It quickly grew in popularity, and in August 1892, a 1,500-foot long wagon and pedestrian bridge was opened from Courtland Beach west across the lake to connect with Ames Avenue in Omaha. Direct electric streetcar service began in 1893 along North 13th Street, with 10-minute service to Locust and North 16th Streets in Omaha. Courtland Beach had a two-story pavilion with room for 2,000, bathhouses for 400 people, and a "gravity road" that was one of the earliest sorts of roller coasters in the Midwest. There was also a large carousel with everything lit up by hundreds of incandescent bulbs.

14,000 people went to Courtland Beach for the Fourth of July in 1895 and watched a female "aeronaut" ascend into the sky by balloon and then jump out with a parachute.

*The view of Nebraska looking across Carter Lake from Wavecrest Park in Carter Lake, Iowa.*

In time, resorts like those at Krug Park and at Lake Manawa took away Courtland's luster. The former amusement park eventually became the private Carter Lake Club. In the 1990s, what remained was developed into residential properties. Today there is the city park called Wavecrest with a small beach and boat launch that offers some of the relaxation Courtland Beach provided over 130 years ago.

## SITE OF COURTLAND BEACH

**What:** A public park on the site of a historic amusement park

**Where:** 112 Shoreline Dr. in Carter Lake, Iowa

**Cost:** Free to visit during daylight hours

**Pro Tip:** On the north shore is Levi Carter Park at 3100 Abbott Dr., which features facilities built during the Great Depression by the CCC and was the site of the Pleasure Pier/Kiddieland amusement park from 1949 to 1959.

# THE MILITARY ROAD

## What happened to the old western trails?

Omaha's modern Military Avenue cuts a diagonal across the city northwest through all sorts of neighborhoods. It had its start when the federal government authorized the construction of an improved and designated overland route between Omaha and the US Army post at Fort Kearney far out on the Great Plains. Much of the route used by the military west of present day Military Road and North 108th Street was better known as the Mormon Trail or California Trail, depending on who was traveling, and likely had many names before that. In 1857 and 1858, Captain Edward Beckwith and a military attachment set out to mark an improved route west from Omaha. The Military Road made its way along the high country, more likely for the ease of wagon travel than from fear of Native American attack. One early place of notoriety along the Military Road on the city's outskirts was the Robber's Roost road ranch. Its unsavory reputation didn't improve after it became the First and Last Chance saloon.

In the city, the old wagon trail became Military Avenue and was the route of the electric streetcars that ran northwest to Benson. During the 1920s, most of Military Avenue was paved in Omaha, where it remains an interesting interruption in the city's typical grid pattern. Further west, the route is still called Military

## AN OLD WEST TRAIL

**What:** 1857 road designated by the US Army

**Where:** Military Ave. northwest from Hamilton St. to the Blair High Rd. and then Military Rd. north and northwest to Bennington Ave.

**Cost:** Free to visit during daylight hours

**Pro Tip:** A small marker for the Oregon and California Trails was erected in 1912 on Military Rd. just west of N. 90th St.

*A rural stretch of Military Road adjacent to Blair High Road.*

Road and leads through suburban subdivisions before ending in the farmlands at Military Road and Bennington Avenue just east of North 204th Street.

A portion of the original wagon road near North 82nd and Fort Streets was placed on the National Register of Historic Places in 1993.

# ASARCO

## Where was the world's largest lead smelter?

At one time, the Omaha riverfront was home to the world's largest lead smelter, which pumped out hellish and noxious plumes of pollution for over a century. It started in 1870 with the Omaha Smelting Company and the raw ore shipped from western mines by the newly completed Union Pacific Railroad. The smelter at 500 Douglas Street would employ 250 men by 1880. Most of the workers were immigrants, and 14 different languages were spoken there. The riverfront smelter later became part of the American Smelting & Refining Company and by 1914 was the largest lead smelter in the world. As of 1924, 165,000 tons of lead and 198,000 ounces of gold were smelted in Omaha, along with many tons of antimonial lead and refined bismuth. Such industries were pointed to with pride as solid symbols of the local economy.

Things were different by the late 20th century. In 1972 came the first reports about exactly how much lead was getting pumped into Omaha's atmosphere. Three years later, the company became known as ASARCO Incorporated, but their operations on the Missouri River at Omaha continued. It wasn't until the 1990s that the company admitted that over 403.9 tons of toxic emissions had been released from the Omaha smelter just since 1987. The smelter was finally closed in 1997 and redeveloped into a 23-acre park named Lewis and Clark

## ONCE THE WORLD'S LARGEST SMELTER

**What:** A sculpture on the site of a smelter

**Where:** Lewis and Clark Landing is at 345 Riverfront Dr.

**Cost:** Free to visit during daylight hours

**Pro Tip:** The nearby National Park Service regional headquarters at 601 Riverfront Dr. is home to Omaha's National Lewis and Clark Historic Trail Visitor Center. Call 402-661-1804 for more information.

*The sculpture* Labor *along the Omaha riverfront.*

Landing. To honor the location's industrial past, the monument *Labor* by Omaha artist Matthew Placzek was dedicated there. The old smelter proved the worst, but not the only, source of the city's lead problems. In 1999, the EPA designated a 29-square-mile area of Omaha as a Superfund site and set about removing and replacing the soil from over 13,000 residential properties between 1999 and 2015.

*Labor* earned iconic status during the Missouri River flood of 2011 when the raised hand of the blacksmith holding the hammer remained visible above the floodwaters.

# CALIFORNIA STREET

## Can you walk right down the middle of the street?

It was one of Omaha's earliest streets, with an optimistic name evoking the West. In 1866, California Street went only as far west as North 25th Street. As the city grew, the thoroughfare became primarily residential with a commercial district around North 16th Street. The 1878 opening of what was originally Creighton College at North 24th Street changed the street and the neighborhood. Creighton would grow into one of the Midwest's preeminent Jesuit universities, and in 1887 California Street was paved between North 16th and North 22nd. That was also when the cornerstone was laid for St. John's Catholic Church, designed by Omaha architect P.J. Creedon. In July 1920, residents were aghast at plans to open an undertaking business at 2103 California Street, according to the *Omaha Bee*. They cited the depressing influence and disease potential in a court injunction and accused the undertakers of opening up without warning

## A STREET WITH NO CARS

**What:** A pedestrian walkway along a former city street

**Where:** On the campus of Creighton University

**Cost:** Free to visit during daylight hours with limited parking

**Pro Tip:** The Creighton Bluejays athletic schedule can be found at https://gocreighton.com/calendar

Creighton Law School graduate Ernie Chambers is Nebraska's longest serving legislator and was in office from 1971 to 2009 and again from 2013 to 2020.

*Modern views of California Street on the Creighton University campus.*

and even "smuggling" a body overnight. The manager told the newspaper, "We can't help it if people die at night."

Creighton University now covers 140 acres, and what was once 10 blocks of California Street is a pedestrian walkway across campus. The eastern end is anchored by Morrison Stadium. On the west at North 27th Plaza is the Heaney Pedestrian Bridge, which opened in 2018 west over the busy North Freeway to connect with the Atlas, the apartment complex in the former St. Joseph Hospital.

THE BIKE UNION AND COFFEE (page 146)

**MT. VERNON GARDENS** (page 70)

**THE GREEKTOWN RIOT** (page 114)

**A GARDEN WITH THE ZODIAC** (page 8)

**CALIFORNIA STREET** (page 86)

ASARCO (page 84)

BRANDEIS (page 122)

**ARISTOTLE IN OMAHA** (page 22)

**THE SINGING TOWER OF WESTLAWN** (page 156)

**A ROLLERCOASTER DISASTER** (page 38)

**PRETTIEST MILE** (page 34)

**BEADLE'S ROCK BROOK CLAIM** (page 46)

**HUMMEL PARK** (page 68)

**THE RESTING PLACE OF OMAHA KID** (page 150)

# LOWERING THE STREETS

## Why is there a door way up there?

Everyone knows the Midwest is flat as a pancake, and the name Nebraska comes from the Otoe word "Flat Water" in reference to the Platte River. Omaha, however, has a few hills even if some aren't quite as steep as they used to be. The city carried out a truly ambitious project in fits and starts through the decades and significantly lowered the grade of the city's streets. By 1906, an estimated million dollars had already been spent on the project, and Farnam Street had been lowered 30-40 feet. The 1906 sale of the Haney homestead at Farnam and South 18th Street marked the end of what the *Omaha Bee* called downtown's "aerial homes" perched on a "yellow clay crag, towering high above the level of the street, and mounted by long flights of steps, usually unpainted"

Toward the end of World War I Omaha began lowering Dodge Street and left behind an unusual example of this massive project. When work started at 20th and Dodge Streets in 1919, it uncovered the "shift wheel house" and cables left from the Omaha Cable Tramway. That was one earlier solution to the terrain as Omaha had downtown cable cars from late 1887 until early 1895. The grading work also left the former front door of St. Mary Magdalene Catholic Church 20 feet up in the air. St. Mary Magdalene had started as a German immigrant parish, and the present church building was constructed in

Senator Robert F. Kennedy attended Mass at St. Mary Magdalene in 1968 a month before he was assassinated.

*St. Mary Magdalene at 19th and Dodge Streets.*

1902. The lowering of Dodge Street presented a peculiar problem solved by Omaha architect John Latenser, Sr., who designed a new basement and first-story underneath the old church. By 1920, Dodge Street at 20th was 36 feet lower than it had been in 1880.

## THE HILLS WERE STEEPER

**What:** A former church front door left up in the air

**Where:** 109 S. 19th St.

**Cost:** Free to view during daylight hours

**Pro Tip:** Omaha had cable cars and also simple streetcars pulled by horses along tracks. Today, for a horse-drawn carriage ride downtown visit https://www.mjcarriage.com/

# THE FLORENCE MILL

## What was Nebraska's oldest industry?

A place to grind a farmer's crops into flour and cornmeal seemed essential to any frontier community, and the Mormon's Winter Quarters was no different. Brigham Young is said to have funded the 1846 construction of a water-powered mill on what became known as Mill Creek. This mill had two burrs for grinding as well as an attached saw for lumber. The shell was all that remained after 1848 when Winter Quarters was abandoned. A Mormon named Alexander Hunter rebuilt the mill in 1856 using the hand-hewn walnut and cottonwood timbers salvaged from the old Mormon mill.

The mill's next owners were German immigrants Jacob and Amalia Weber, who settled in Florence in 1857 shortly after their marriage. They operated it as a water-powered sawmill and by 1861 had six employees and produced 65,000 board feet of lumber. The emphasis had shifted to grain by 1880, and by 1888 the mill was powered by steam. The 53-foot grain elevator was added in 1913, when the mill was converted to a feed mill for livestock. Jacob Weber continued at the mill until his death at age 90 in 1923. His son Jacob Jr. then took over and the mill was upgraded again to electrical power. The mill passed to 18-year-old Lyman Weber in 1931. The Depression years were lean, with constant flooding—including one flood that left the mill standing in 14 feet of water. A successful lawsuit prompted moving the mill away from its location along Mill Creek and out of the floodplain. The mill closed during WWII when Lyman served in the military, but he returned and

The Florence Mill was listed on the National Register of Historic Places in 1998.

*The Florence Mill in 2020.*

continued operations until 1964.
The old mill was then owned by
Ernest and Ruthie Harpster and
was considered Nebraska's oldest
business until it closed in 1990.
Since 1997, the mill has been
operated as the Winter Quarters
Mill Museum and ArtLoft Gallery
by artist Linda Meigs.

## WHERE YOU GOT YOUR GRAIN GROUND

**What:** Art and more in a historic mill

**Where:** 9102 N. 30th St.

**Cost:** Call 402-551-1233 for hours.

**Pro Tip:** The Mill hosts a seasonal farmers market, and the Florence neighborhood celebrates its independent origins at the annual Florence Days. See http://www.historicflorence.org/FlorenceDays.php for dates.

# OMAHA'S EXPOSITIONS AND INDIAN CONGRESS

## What happened when the world came to Omaha?

There was a time when Americans were enthralled by grand expositions, and a World's Fair sure seemed something to see. Omaha hosted two late-19th-century expositions, in 1898 and again in 1899, that showcased the city and all the possibilities of the West. All the effort that went into hosting these expositions was intended to boost the city out of the hard times of the early 1890s. What America, and Omaha, really needed was a grand celebration about themselves. Omaha businessman Gurdon Wattles shaped what became the Trans-Mississippi and International Exposition and Indian Congress in 1898. The five-month event took place during the Spanish-American War amidst a patriotic hoopla that made it even more popular. More than two and a half million people visited the 180 acre Exposition grounds, including President William McKinley. There were exhibits from across the West along with such attractions as the Streets of Cairo, the Midway, Buffalo Bill, and grand classical buildings—built out of horse-hair plaster—that lined a 2,000-foot-long lagoon.

The Exposition also brought together the Indian Congress, which was promoted by Captain W. A. Mercer as the last gathering of America's Native peoples—as though they were intended to just disappear. Forty thousand dollars were

The Giant See-Saw from the Omaha Expositions ended up at Coney Island's Luna Park in New York City.

*Historic marker and baseball diamond at Kountze Park.*

appropriated to stage the exhibit, and 500 members of 35 different tribes were present, including the Apache Chief Geronimo. Ethnologist James Mooney was also present, and the promoters encouraged sham battles and even a performance of the Ghost Dance less than a decade after the Wounded Knee massacre. The next year, Omaha hosted the Greater American Exposition, which offered many of the same extravagant wonders but proved less financially successful.

## SITE OF THE TRANS-MISSISSIPPI EXPOSITION

**What:** Site of Expositions in 1898 and 1899.

**Where:** The two historical markers are in Kountze Park at Florence Blvd. and Pinkney St.

**Cost:** Free to visit during daylight hours

**Pro Tip:** You can see a scale model layout of the grounds of the Trans-Mississippi Exposition at the Durham Museum. See https://durhammuseum.org/ for hours and admission.

# WINTER QUARTERS

## When was Omaha filled with religious refugees?

In early 1846, thousands of Mormons set out from their former headquarters at Nauvoo, Illinois. Earlier troubles had already forced members of the Latter-day Saints to leave Ohio and then Missouri. The 1844 murder of their prophet Joseph Smith sent them out again, headed west across Iowa. After Mormon leader Brigham Young came to an agreement with the Omaha Nation, a community was organized made up of tents, log cabins, and crude shelters dug into the bluffs. This was Winter Quarters which by Christmas had a population of some 3,500 Mormons, who suffered hunger and rampant disease.

The area's timber and game were depleted, causing tensions with their Omaha landlords. Forced from their homes upriver in the Blackbird Hills, the Omaha struggled in the face of starvation, dislocation, and continued depredations. John Miller, the Omaha's government agent, feared that Winter Quarters was intended as a

A 1936 sculpture by Avard Fairbanks at 3100 State Street commemorates the estimated 350 Mormon pioneers who died and were buried at Winter Quarters.

*The Winter Quarters memorial in Florence Park.*

permanent way-station for Mormon converts coming from the East and Europe and he therefore forced them to leave. Brigham Young damned Milller's bones to hell, but in May 1848, the Mormons deserted Winter Quarters. Church activities relocated east across the Missouri River to Kanesville, now modern Council Bluffs.

For many years, a giant cottonwood in the park was referred to as Brigham Young's tree, with stories that he either planted it, used it as a hitching post, or had nothing to do with it whatsoever. The tree died between 1947 and 1950, and the stump was removed as a hazard.

# THE GREEKTOWN RIOT

## How does hate turn on a neighborhood?

It started in February 1909 with complaining neighbors and an altercation in a rented room above a shoe store at N and South 24th Streets. Greek immigrant John Masourides was caught with a 17-year-old "American" girl named Lillian Breese. He was there to learn English. Instead, he was arrested for vagrancy by South Omaha police officer Ed Lowrey. Officer Lowrey was a 42-year-old Irish immigrant who had joined the South Omaha police after losing his job during a packinghouse strike. Masourides was disarmed of his knife, but apparently not his gun. There was a tussle on the street, and Lowrey was shot and died.

Masourides ran only to be apprehended again. The police would not swear the gun discovered in his room was the same one turned in. Out of concerns about a possible lynching, Masourides was taken to the Douglas County Jail and then the Omaha police station.

In South Omaha, orators that included two Nebraska legislators whipped up a crowd of some 500 people that then set upon Greektown. Two 15-year-olds were injured by a shotgun fired into the crowd as 50 buildings were demolished, mostly along Q Street between South 24th and South 28th Streets. Hundreds fled as other immigrant victims included four Polish laborers, Italians, and an unnamed Romanian rescued from a beating at Q and South 30th Street. One destroyed home stood less than 100 feet from the South Omaha police station.

The United States eventually paid $40,000 in indemnities to the Kingdom of Greece and the Ottoman and Austro-Hungarian Empires over the 1909 South Omaha Riot.

*The southwest corner of South 24th and N Streets.*

Another was an apartment at I and South 28th Streets where 25 or 30 Greek immigrants lived. In Council Bluffs, the police rounded up 300 Greek men, disarmed them, and promised protection, food, and shelter. Masourides spent five years in prison and was then deported.

## ANTI-IMMIGRANT RIOT

**What:** Site of a 1909 riot against Greek immigrants

**Where:** Intersection of N and S. 24th Sts.

**Cost:** Free to visit during daylight hours

**Pro Tip:** After 2004, the intersection of N and S. 24th became better known for the people watching Plaza de la Raza while work progressed on four surrounding murals dedicated to the heritage of the neighborhood's more recent Mexican, Salvadoran, Honduran, and Guatemalan immigrants.

# THE PRAGUE HOTEL

## Who promoted Praha?

There are no more nightly rooms or beef with dill gravy these days, but the stout brick Prague Hotel still stands in the heart of Omaha's old "Bohemia Town" or *Praha*. The unlikely origins of Nebraska's large Czech immigrant population can be traced to Ed Rosewater, a Czech Jewish immigrant who became a telegrapher. That's what brought him to Omaha, where he started the newspapers the *Omaha Daily Bee*, the *Pokrok Zapadu* in Czech, and the German *Beobachter am Missouri*. The fiery Rosewater would become a political force who likely helped Tom Dennison enter politics. All the while, Omaha's Czech neighborhood grew along South 10th west to South 16th Streets between Pierce south to Martha Streets.

Vaclav Stepanek had a Czech dance hall on a site that was eventually acquired by the Omaha Brewing Association. That was Omaha beer baron Gottlieb Storz's company, and German immigrant architect Joseph Guth was hired to design a new hotel where only Storz beer would be

### OMAHA'S CZECH HOTEL

**What:** A historic hotel in Omaha's Czech neighborhood

**Where:** 1402 S. 13th St.

**Cost:** Free to view during daylight hours

**Pro Tip:** The famed Sokol Auditorium at 2234 S. 13th St. has hosted concerts from Primus and Pennywise to locals like Cursive and 311, so check out http://sokolauditorium.com/ to see what's coming up.

While working as a telegrapher for the War Department, Ed Rosewater was the one who first sent news of the Emancipation Proclamation over the wire.

*The Prague Hotel on South 13th Street in 2020.*

served. The 25-room Prague Hotel opened in 1898 and advertised in the *Bee* newspaper "Board and room, $4.50 up: steam heat." Notably, the hotel restaurant's kitchen was in the basement.

In 1915 Joseph Pivonka took over the hotel. During the 1930s, the WPA's Guide to Omaha called the Prague's restaurant the only restaurant between Chicago and the West Coast that "specializes in Bohemian dishes, shrimp, frog legs, and steaks." The hotel eventually closed and in 1987 was converted into apartments and listed on the National Register of Historic Places.

# A PABST TIED HOUSE

## Where could a cowboy get a drink?

The remaining block of N Street west of South 26th Avenue no longer bustles the way it once did. The nearby stockyards created the neighborhood, but the 1970s construction of the Kennedy Freeway left it isolated. Still, an original Pabst beer saloon has endured for more than 120 years as everything around has changed. The saloon was constructed as a tied house directly owned by the brewery where their beer would be sold exclusively. This was the era when bars offered a free and often salty lunch to help attract the thirsty crowds, and in February 1899, an Omaha newspaper announced that Pabst had completed its new South Omaha enterprise.

Pabst started out as Empire Brewing in Milwaukee in the 1840s and grew into one of America's largest and best-known breweries. Truly, it was the beer that made Milwaukee famous after German immigrant Frederick Pabst took over, and the name was changed in 1890. The company still exists today, although it's now headquartered in San Antonio, Texas. Pabst Blue Ribbon and Old Milwaukee remain two of its signature brews.

Ownership of the South Omaha Pabst saloon changed through the years. At one time, it was reputedly just one of the gambling joints and brothels operated by neighborhood gangster "Lightnin'" Johnson. Still, a 1972 Environmental

---

### SOUTH OMAHA WATERING HOLE

**What:** An 1899 Pabst tied-house saloon

**Where:** 2613–2615 N St.

**Cost:** Free to view during daylight hours

**Pro Tip:** The craft beer craze swept Omaha the same as elsewhere, and anyone thirsty can find a drink in Omaha these days. Find them all at http://www.omahacraftbrew.com/

*The 1899 Pabst tied house on N Street.*

Impact Statement on highway construction that found only "badly deteriorated" buildings was used to justify the new highway that was deemed to have no effect on "areas of unique interest or scenic beauty".

An original Metz brewery tied-house saloon can be seen at 510 South 10th Street in Omaha's Old Market.

# SCARS OF THE 1919 COURTHOUSE RIOT

## When is a race riot nothing but a swindle?

It was a scam. The riot and the lynching and then burning of William Brown at 18th and Dodge Streets was nothing but a set-up to discredit Mayor Ed Smith's reform administration. It was intended to get Tom Dennison's good old boys back into office and political power. It worked, and "Cowboy Jim" Dahlman was re-elected Mayor of Omaha in 1921.

In 1912 Omahans justly celebrated the completion of the new Douglas County Courthouse. The French Renaissance Revival building was a truly significant structure for the city, and was designed by John Latenser, Sr., an immigrant from Liechtenstein. Bedford stone covered the exterior, and the county jail was originally on the fifth floor. Seven years later, William Brown was incarcerated there before he was taken out and lynched at 18th and Harney Streets. Mayor Smith was almost lynched too. In 1919, during America's "red summer," racial tensions exploded into violence. That year supporters of Tom Dennison dressed in blackface to assault white Omahans on the street, outrageous incidents were reported by the newspapers regardless of whether they really happened, and Agnes Loebeck accused a Black man named William Brown of rape.

Brown suffered from rheumatoid arthritis and couldn't have jumped out of any bushes to beat a boyfriend or rape any woman, as he was alleged to have done. That woman was Ms. Loebeck, and the boyfriend was Dennison associate Milton

The murals above the courthouse rotunda were damaged during the 1919 riot and were restored to their original condition in 2014.

*Exterior and interior of the 1912 Douglas County Courthouse at 1701 Farnam Street.*

Hoffman. Hoffman would help stir up the crowd supplied with all the liquor they wanted who were ferried to and from the courthouse by automobile. In the chaos, $500,000 damage was done, certain tax records were destroyed, and gunshots were fired that left scars visible today.

## COURTHOUSE HISTORY

**What:** Bullet scars from the 1919 Courthouse riot.

**Where:** Look around the rotunda at the Douglas County Courthouse, 1701 Farnam St.

**Cost:** Free to visit during normal business hours with metered parking

**Pro Tip:** The footprints of the 1975 Apollo-Soyuz Test Project astronauts and cosmonauts can be seen in the attached City-County Building, including those of Soviet Commander Alexei Leonov, who became the first human to walk in space in 1965.

# BRANDEIS

## Where could you buy anything?

At one time, every American city had one big department store downtown that was just a bit more fancy than anywhere else. In Omaha, that place was Brandeis. The business that dominated downtown had a humble start in 1881, when a Jewish Czech immigrant named Jonas Brandeis opened The Fair on South 13th Street. Brandeis was born in Prague and turned his name into a household word. In 1888, Brandeis moved on to the Boston Store located at Douglas and South 16th Streets right in the thriving heart of downtown. Eighteen years later, the J. L. Brandeis and Sons Building opened as Omaha's destination downtown department store. The eight-story building cost almost $1 million to construct and was designed by John Latenser, Sr., in the Second Renaissance Revival style. One December 1908 advertisement in the *Bee* newspaper boasted Brandeis had its own post office branch along with "Free Rest Rooms and Waiting rooms for Women and Children," a telephone, delivery service to any depot in Omaha, and daily concerts in the sheet music department. Brandeis also advertised the "Biggest Christmas Display in the West" with "Santa Claus and his Live Educated Dog" and "Thousands of Electric and Mechanical Toys." It was the annual Christmas display that several locals would remember most.

*Exterior details on the South 16th Street side of the Brandeis building.*

Two additional stories were added in 1921 with bargains in the basement and a restaurant up top. Eying the future, Brandeis helped develop the Crossroads shopping mall at 72nd and Dodge Streets in 1959 and then in 1966 the Southroads Mall in Bellevue. At the chain's peak, there were 15 Brandeis department stores. Then the downtown store closed in 1980. Brandeis was sold to Younkers department stores in 1987. The last Younkers closed in 2018. The downtown Brandeis department store was converted into apartments with a small food court and corner convenience store.

The Brandeis Building was listed on the National Register of Historic Places in 1982.

# POTTER'S FIELD

## What happened to the anonymous dead?

This was where the poor and unfortunate were buried. There were unnamed infants and floaters found in the Missouri River and so many others through the years. The county purchased the land from the adjacent Forest Lawn Cemetery Association in 1887. The last burial took place in August 1957. In between, there were almost 4,000 burials there. There was 81-year-old Jacob Smith, who the *Bee* newspaper called "an old-time resident of the city" who died in jail because he had nowhere else to go. There were 1,180 children under the age of two years. The remains of William Brown were laid to rest at Potter's Field after he was lynched in Omaha in 1919.

Like almost everyone buried there, Brown's grave was unmarked and remained that way until 2011. That's when a Californian named Chris Hebert saw a documentary about Henry Fonda. The actor was in Omaha in 1919 and witnessed the lynching. He

A Nebraska historical marker was dedicated at Potter's Field in October 2020.

*Potter's Field on Young Street and a small memorial to those buried here.*

would remember it. Hebert donated the money to get William Brown a stone that includes the inscription "Lest We Forget." That effort brought renewed interest to what had been an ignored and forgotten part of Omaha's history, resulting in the organization of an annual clean-up by volunteers.

# THE OTOE MISSION

## What were Nebraska's first schools like?

This official Nebraska historical marker seems an afterthought left in the continued expansion of US Highway 75 between Bellevue and Plattsmouth. It commemorates a different Nebraska, when the Reverend Moses Merrill opened a Baptist mission to bring Christianity and American civilization to the Otoe and Missouria. Times had not been good. The fur trade and the introduction of alcohol totally disrupted a seasonal lifestyle of farming and hunting. The Otoe's old access to the buffalo that lived to the west and southwest brought them into direct conflict with the Osage, Dakota, Cheyenne, and others. Smallpox came through in late 1831. Their population declined from perhaps 1,200 during the 1820s to 943 in 1840, almost half of whom were children. Starvation became a reality.

That was the Nebraska Merrill and his wife Eliza found when they arrived at Bellevue in 1833. He was from Maine, and she was from New York, and they got married in Michigan before they became the area's first permanent missionaries. Even with their own agenda, missionaries like the Merrills provided a counterpoint to the traders' endless greed and alcohol. They moved closer to the Otoe in 1835, but their first mission burned. The second one was a home with enough room for church services and a school for Otoe children.

## THE MERRILL MISSION

**What:** Historical marker for a Baptist mission

**Where:** S. 10th St. south of Pinecrest Rd. in La Platte

**Cost:** Free to visit during daylight hours

**Pro Tip:** Access to the 8.9 mile Bellevue Loop Trail can be found just north of US Highway 34 on Harlan Lewis Rd., and the trail is due to re-open in 2021 with an interesting look along Papillion Creek near the point where it flows into the Missouri River.

*Historic marker for the Merrill's Baptist mission along US Highway 75 south of Bellevue.*

Times got worse with no game left locally or elsewhere. In April 1837, Chief Ietan was killed in a factional dispute as Otoe society all but fell apart. That September, the Merrills buried their only child. Reverend Merrill contracted tuberculosis in 1839 and died the next year. Eliza returned east and opened an orphanage in Albany. The Otoe-Missouria Tribe is now headquartered in Red Rock, Oklahoma.

Merrill published Nebraska's first book in 1834, a hymn book in Otoe named *Wdtwhtl Wdwdklha Tva Eva Wdhonetl.*

# OMAHA'S MAIN STREET

## How far west will Omaha go?

Unlike most western towns, Omaha lacked an official Main Street. That all changed in the early 21st century when the town of Elkhorn was annexed. At the time, Elkhorn had perhaps 8,000 people. As had happened in Millard and Dundee, the annexation brought courtroom controversy that resulted in some hurt feelings. In the end, the courts ruled Elkhorn was legally annexed, and in March 2007, it ceased to exist after 142 years.

The annexation would surely have been a wonder to the railroad workers who built the Union Pacific west through an ocean of prairie grass. It was originally called Elkhorn Station and appeared alongside the railroad tracks two miles east of the Elkhorn River. The new town was platted in 1867, when Omaha was at least 25 miles away. In 1874 the *Bee* newspaper reported the village included two general stores and harness makers McKrather & Bartlet, and the Schmeck House had been "refitted" into a restaurant. J. B Silvis, "proprietor of the UP photograph car," had plans in the works to build a two-story brick store and hall. Based in Elkhorn, Silvis would document much of this era by way of his modified boxcar fitted with living quarters and a darkroom. Elkhorn was a "flourishing village" according to Johnson's 1880 *History of Nebraska*, with "large grain warehouses" as the town served as an "extensive shipping point for grain and produce."

---

### DOWNTOWN ELKHORN

**What:** Old downtown of the former Elkhorn, Nebraska

**Where:** N. Main St. between Railroad Ave. and Corby St.

**Cost:** Free to visit during daylight hours.

**Pro Tip:** South of downtown Elkhorn, across the tracks and then east on E. Park Rd., are three miles of 1920s brick-paved Lincoln Highway, the longest remaining stretch in America.

*Looking north on North Main Street. Photograph courtesy of Michaela Armetta.*

Elkhorn developed as more of a typical, small Nebraska farm town and had a population of only 476 by 1960. Suburbia and aggressive annexation in the 1990s grew Elkhorn from 1,400 people to over 6,000 in 10 years. Omaha began annexation in 2005.

The Post Office at Elkhorn was originally named Chicago.

# THE BLOCKHOUSE AND MISSION

## Where did Father De Smet get his start?

These two markers signify a place that no longer really exists as the protruding bluff located here was hauled away long ago. In the 1830s, the Potawatomi and a few Chippewa and Ottawa allies were removed to a western Iowa reservation. The 1832 Treaty of Tippecanoe had diminished their lands, and by the terms of the Treaty of Chicago, a year later they agreed to move west. As encouragement, the American government would build a mill and a farm worked by a government employee. There was also to be a fortification, and in 1837 Captain D. B. Moore and the 1st Regiment of US Dragoons constructed a blockhouse on the now vanished bluff overlooking the Indian Creek valley. In the 1830s, that was the location of the Potawatomi settlement where Billy Caldwell lived. Half-Irish and half-Mohawk, Caldwell typically served as the Potawatomi's collective representative in dealing with the Americans, although he wasn't a chief in the traditional sense.

The next year the blockhouse was given to Catholic missionaries, among them the Belgian Jesuit Pierre-Jean De Smet on his first foray into the West. De Smet believed they'd find several hundred Catholics when they arrived, but the 2,000 Potawatomi that met them seemed mostly uninterested in their religion. Undaunted, St. Joseph's Mission was established at the blockhouse with a school for children that fall. De Smet

Billy Caldwell was a Captain in the British Indian Service and served as the first judge in Peoria County, Illinois.

*Looking southwest on East Pierce Street in Council Bluffs, Iowa.*

wrote that bears were "not uncommon," and wolves stole their chickens. He was also horrified by the rampant alcohol-induced violence. De Smet left St. Joseph's in 1840 to continue his work farther west. Billy Caldwell died in 1841, and St. Joseph's Mission closed soon after. In 1846, the Potawatomi began to move to a new reservation where the Prairie Band Potawatomi are still headquartered in Mayetta, Kansas.

## A CATHOLIC MISSION

**What:** Markers for a Jesuit mission and a US Blockhouse

**Where:** The southeast side of Pierce St. between Franklin Ave. and Union St.

**Cost:** Free to visit during daylight hours with nearby parking

**Pro Tip:** The nearby 100 Block of West Broadway offers several bars and restaurants and was listed on the National Register of Historic Places in 2002.

# DEBOLT

## Why did some places thrive while others didn't?

Modern Omaha now includes once-independent towns like Millard and Dundee, along with a few places that never developed their own identity. This latter group would include DeBolt. The area that became DeBolt was all rural Douglas County in 1872 when there were finally enough local farmers to justify the opening of the Springville country school. Many of the farmers were Scandinavian immigrants. In 1887 came the construction of a Fremont, Missouri Valley & Elkhorn Railroad branch line between Omaha and Arlington with connections to South Omaha and to the Chicago, St. Paul, Minneapolis & Omaha Railroad line. New stations were established at Debolt as well as at Irvington and Bennington. Like other new towns alongside the tracks, DeBolt became a local shipping point for cattle and grain. A post office was opened in 1892 but closed just seven years later.

The railroad line through DeBolt was absorbed into the Chicago & North Western railroad by 1903, even as Irvington and Bennington overshadowed DeBolt as a shipping point. Instead of growing, DeBolt seemed to mostly fade away. However, it retained enough of a sense of community in July 1919 to protest Omaha's plan to establish a garbage dump on a nearby farm. The area was annexed into

## A FORGOTTEN TOWN AND HISTORIC CEMETERY

**What:** A rural Danish cemetery now surrounded by Omaha.

**Where:** DeBolt was between N. 56th and N. 60th Sts. between Craig and Read Sts. Springwell Cemetery is at 6326 Hartman Ave.

**Cost:** Free to visit during daylight hours

**Pro Tip:** Not too far from DeBolt there's what looks like someone's house, but it is really home to the wonderful Mangia Italiana restaurant at 6516 Irvington Rd.

*Springwell Danish Cemetery on Hartman Avenue. Photograph courtesy of Michaela Armetta.*

Omaha in the 1950s, and the railroad line that brought DeBolt to existence was abandoned in the 1970s.

One reminder of this community is the nearby Springwell Danish Cemetery just south of the town site. The cemetery was established in 1887 on ten acres and is known for the many Danish immigrants and their descendants buried here, with some of the gravestone inscriptions in Danish. The cemetery became an Omaha Landmark in 1996. The surrounding farms have long since been subdivided into suburban neighborhoods as the once rural Danish cemetery and railroad stop at DeBolt became part of Omaha.

The Fremont, Elkhorn & Missouri Valley Railroad's "Cowboy Line" across northern Nebraska is now the 321-mile-long Cowboy Trail between Columbus and Chadron.

# MONUMENTS TO STOCKYARDS

## Where was the world's largest livestock market?

It all started in 1883 after a group of investors bought up 2,000 acres south of Omaha.

The Union Stockyards covered 300 acres, and the rest was platted into the City of South Omaha. By 1890, South Omaha had a population of 8,000, and everyone called it the "Magic City" due to its explosive and sudden growth. The stockyards were soon surrounded by massive meatpacking plants and neighborhoods of mostly immigrant workers. During the 1890s, the "Big Four" meatpacking plants were Cudahy, Swift, Armour, and Wilson, and there were smaller packers and businesses in everything from leather and lard to glue. "Packingtown" employed 5,000 workers by 1892. The railroads and later trucks brought the cattle, hogs, and sheep from across the West. By 1897, the Armour meatpacking plant in South Omaha was the largest in the world.

South Omaha had a population of 40,000 when it was annexed in 1915 as one of the nation's major centers of livestock production. By 1921, 13,000 people worked at the packinghouses, where over 921,000 cattle and almost two million hogs had been turned into meat the year before. The imposing Livestock Exchange Building was constructed in 1926. It was designed by Omaha architect George Prinz and still dominates the South O skyline.

---

The Omaha Stockyards was the world's largest livestock market from 1955 to 1971.

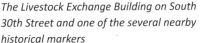

*The Livestock Exchange Building on South 30th Street and one of the several nearby historical markers*

Decentralization, environmental restrictions, and nonunion labor took the packers out of urban centers like Omaha as they closed one after another. In 1999, the original odoriferous institution closed as the stockyards were replaced with a business park and South Omaha campus of Metropolitan Community College. The old Exchange was converted into housing.

## THE STOCKYARDS

**What:** Series of panels about the history of South Omaha

**Where:** Near the former Livestock Exchange at 4920 S. 30th St.

**Cost:** Free to visit during daylight hours

**Pro Tip:** The stockyards meant the best steaks anywhere, and there are still a few of the old Omaha style steakhouses left, with Johnny's Cafe right at 4702 S. 27th St. along with Gorat's at 4917 Center St., and The Drover at 2121 S. 73rd St.

# THE IOWA SCHOOL FOR THE DEAF

## How can a school foster a culture?

On the southeast edge of Council Bluffs sits the campus of one of the Omaha metropolitan area's most historic educational institutions. The Iowa School for the Deaf (I.S.D.) moved to Council Bluffs in 1870. I.S.D. was intended to be self-sustaining, with its own farm, dairy, and power plant where students could gain a variety of educational and vocational skills.

The entire history of America's treatment of its deaf citizens played out in Council Bluffs while a significant local community developed. In 1901, Council Bluffs resident Dr. J. Schuyler Long's *Manual of the Sign Language* was advertised for sale in the *American Annals of the Deaf*. As elsewhere, Council Bluffs developed its own dialect of American Sign Language. Fires in

## A MUSEUM OF EDUCATION

**What:** A museum dedicated to the history of the Iowa School for the Deaf

**Where:** 3501 Harry Langdon Blvd. in Council Bluffs.

**Cost:** Contact 712-366-0571 for current hours and cost.

**Pro Tip:** Southwest across the road from I.S.D. is the trailhead of the Wabash Trace, a rail-to-trail that follows 63 miles of the former route of the Wabash railroad's *Cannonball* between Council Bluffs and Blanchard on the Missouri state line.

The Nebraska School for the Deaf operated in Omaha from 1869 until 1998, with the former campus at 3223 North 45th Street.

*Buildings at the Iowa School for the Deaf, including the Administration Building and the wing housing the I.S.D. Museum.*

1892 and again in 1902 altered the I.S.D. campus, which seemed less isolated with its own electric streetcar line from 1909 until 1931. The next year, high school diplomas accredited by the State of Iowa were first issued to students. The largest graduating class was in 1984, 18 years after a rubella epidemic. At that time there were almost 400 students on campus.

Today, the museum at I.S.D. features a variety of artifacts from the school's history, including nine gravestones from when the campus cemetery was relocated due to highway construction. A walk around the tree-shaded campus features historic panels that commemorate the Mormon Grand Encampment of 1846 and the Mormon Battalion, reputedly the longest military march in American history.

# DEPOT ON THE OMAHA ROAD

## Who took the last train from Florence?

This train stop now stands up on a hill, well away from the tracks where it started, but there's still an Omaha Road depot up in Florence. Officially this was the Chicago, St. Paul, Minneapolis & Omaha Railway, but that's more than a mouthful. The railroad started out back in 1869 as a local enterprise by well-known businessmen called the Omaha & Northwestern, with tracks built north from Omaha through Blair and Herman to Sioux City. The railroad ran right through Florence, but the trains did not stop there. The Omaha Road took over in 1881, and in 1887 a Florence depot was finally built at North 28th Avenue and Grebe Street. In July of the same year, a young unmarried woman in the neighborhood named Huldah Nelson, who'd just given birth, had Florence railroad hand James Donohoe arrested as the father.

At its peak, the Omaha Road covered 1,700 miles and connected Omaha and the suburban Florence depot to the Twin Cities, Chicago, and a few branch lines as well. This was one of the "granger railroads" largely dependent on hauling crops from small stations to larger terminals for processing or export, as well as traffic from depots like the one at Florence.

Effective control passed to the Chicago & North Western railroad as the Omaha Road was operated as a subsidiary until

The northern terminus in Florence for the O&CB electric streetcars was at North 30th and Filmore Streets.

*The Florence depot on North 30th Street.*

it was officially merged in 1972. The depot at Florence had already closed down in 1966. Most such depots were soon razed. This one was saved and in 1971 was relocated to its present location. In 1976, the restored Florence Omaha Road depot was opened as a museum showcasing the locality's rich history.

## HISTORIC RAILROAD DEPOT

**What:** An Omaha Road railroad depot

**Where:** 9000 N. 30th St.

**Cost:** Free but contact 402-453-4280 for current hours of operation

**Pro Tip:** There's a nearby historical marker in honor of WWI General John J. Pershing alongside the M.U.D. trail. The trail is accessible at 8101 John J. Pershing Dr. and the monument is to the south. It was erected on Armistice Day 1941, less than a month before the start of WWII.

# THE GANGSTER AND THE ARCHITECT

## How can crime pay?

Jack Broomfield was from Savannah, Missouri, and had lost a leg while working as a Pullman porter before he showed up in Omaha in 1887. Broomfield would soon find a comfortable place in Tom Dennison's political machine and was dubbed "supreme dictator of negro politics in Omaha" by a Lincoln newspaper. Broomfield took over the Midway at North 12th Street and Capitol Avenue. The *Bee* newspaper called the Midway a nationally known "saloon, dance hall, and gambling resort" that catered to African-Americans. There were drinks and all the gambling games available at what suffragist Elizabeth Cady Stanton once called the "most notorious dive in Omaha." Broomfield also took over the four-story Castle at 116-118 South 9th Street, which was advertised as a hotel for Blacks. All the while, Broomfield worked to get Omaha's Black community to vote for the candidates who would keep the machine in power.

After the devastation of the 1913 Easter tornado, Broomfield hired a young Omaha architect named Clarence Wigington. Wigington worked under Thomas Kimball and had submitted the rowhouse design to *Good Housekeeping* magazine in 1909. It won first prize, and it subsequently became a reality on Lake Street. Wigington would go on to further acclaim after leaving Omaha; he served for 34 years as America's first black municipal architect while senior designer for St. Paul, Minnesota.

According to political Boss Tom Dennison, Jack Broomfield was "true blue and always loyal."

*The Broomfield apartments on Lake Street.*

Prohibition shuttered the Midway in 1917. In 1921 Charleu Broomfield sued Jack for divorce citing "extreme cruelty." By then, Broomfield operated a drug store at 111 South 14th Street. He died in 1927, and Tom Dennison served as one of his pallbearers.

## HISTORIC HOME

**What:** A 1913 rowhouse designed by a prominent architect

**Where:** 2502–2504 Lake St.

**Cost:** Free to view during daylight hours

**Pro Tip:** Another nearby building designed by Clarence Wigington is the Zion Baptist Church, located at 2215 Grant St.

# MARKER FOR THE MAINLINE

## How can a railroad create a community?

The residents don't pronounce the name the same as the French fur traders did, but today's bustling small city of Papillion appeared on the north bank of Little Papillion Creek soon after the Union Pacific railroad was completed in 1869. The new town was in Sarpy County on the Union Pacific's original main line. That route was largely determined due to the machinations of Dr. Thomas Durant, who manipulated railroad stocks and created Crédit Mobilier to reap outrageous profits for constructing the transcontinental railroad. The 1869 route originally made a peculiar loop southwest of Omaha that added nine miles and seemed mostly intended to gain more land and money from the federal government. Such unorthodox methods seemingly put Dr. Durant into conflict with General Grenville Dodge, the railroad's chief surveyor, but the two might have also made money together smuggling cotton out of the Confederacy. The Crédit Mobilier scandal broke in 1872 and soon infected the administration of President U.S. Grant and his allies in Congress. Dr. Durant spent the last years of his life fighting all the lawsuits against him.

As for Papillion, John Beadle pre-empted the land in 1857 when he met, but proved to be no relation to, the dime-novel publisher. His brother constructed Papillion's first building in November 1869, and the town was platted two months later.

---

Actor Colm Meany portrayed Dr. Thomas Durant on the AMC television series *Hell on Wheels*.

*The historical marker and Sump Library looking south on North Washington Street in Papillion*

The Sarpy County courthouse was moved from Bellevue to Papillion in 1875. In 1908, the railroad moved out of downtown Papillion when the Union Pacific route was straightened by the Lane Cut-off. The small town's population has grown from just over 1,000 people in 1950 to over 20,000 according to latest census estimates.

## RAILROAD HISTORY

**What:** Historical marker for the Union Pacific Railroad's original main line

**Where:** At the Sump Library at 222 N. Jefferson St. in Papillion

**Cost:** Free to visit during daylight hours

**Pro Tip:** Adjacent to the library at 242 Franklin St. sits the relocated Portal School. The one-room schoolhouse was open from 1890 until 1993 at Portal, a ghost town located between Papillion and Millard. In 1995 the schoolhouse was purchased and moved by the Papillion Area Historical Society.

# AK-SAR-BEN AIR FIELD

## When did they fly mail through the air?

A lost airfield with a role in the early days of aviation is now commemorated by a state historical marker next to a university parking lot. For a few years during the early days of airplanes, Ak-Sar-Ben Field was an important place. The Knights of Ak-Sar-Ben charitable group purchased the former state fairground in 1919 to use as a horse-racing track. At the same time, the Chamber of Commerce worked to develop an adjacent airfield and built a hangar at what is now South 63rd and Center Streets. Ak-Sar-Ben Field came into prominence during the October 1919 Transcontinental Air Race, which proved an airmail route across the country was possible. Airmail started between Omaha and Chicago in May 1920 with the transcontinental mail route, in service between New York City and San Francisco beginning that September.

In those barnstorming days, pilots were daredevils with a death wish. In May 1919, two pilots were badly injured attempting to land when their plane stalled at 300 feet and

## EARLY AIRPORT

**What:** Nebraska marker for a historic airfield

**Where:** S. 67th and Williams Sts.

**Cost:** Free to visit during daylight hours with limited parking

**Pro Tip:** Nearby Stinson Park at 2285 S. 67th St. is home to the Maha Music Festival and several other concerts, an annual farmers market, and a monument to the racehorse Omaha, who won the Triple Crown in 1935. See http://aksarbenvillage.com for more.

Nine men were killed during the 1919 Transcontinental Air Race

*The historic marker for Ak-Sar-Ben Field on South 67th Street.*

nosedived to the ground while hundreds watched. The *Bee* reported in June 1920, a plane "swooped down out of the clouds, and the pilot leaped from his seat leaving his motor running" at Ak-Sar-Ben Field. The pilot was former Council Bluffs minister A.J. Nielsen, who ran down and beat up airplane mechanic Jack Kirk and then jumped back into his plane and flew away. Nielsen claimed Kirk was a former employee who had been talking ill of him.

The air mail moved to Fort Crook in 1924, and a tornado damaged the hangar. Ak-Sar-Ben Field only lasted a handful of years while horse racing continued nearby until 1995.

# FUTURISM, BICYCLES, AND COFFEE

### Is that a flying saucer?

The 1960s was a decade of future promise and social chaos, and Omaha was no exception. The 1966 demolition of both Omaha's Old City Hall at South 18th and Farnam Streets and the imposing 1890s Post Office at 16th and Dodge Streets sparked serious questions about downtown's direction and led to the first local preservation efforts. There were still plenty of smokestacks downtown during the 1960s, even as many residents moved farther west.

A contrast to Omaha's old soot-stained brick buildings would be sleek structures of a more modern sort with plenty of glass. One of Omaha's more interesting examples from this period can be found on the corner of 19th and Dodge Streets. Over the years, the building has been compared to a cupcake, a flying saucer, and maybe something stolen from the futuristic cartoon show *The Jetsons*. It might have even been meant to resemble Mercury's helmet. The unusual building was constructed in 1968 as a bank branch. The architect of this novel bit of downtown 1960s futurism was Nes Latenser of the famed Omaha architectural firm John Latenser & Sons.

The building sat vacant after 2011. Elsewhere, many such remnants of 1960s modernism seemed inefficient and sometimes downright ugly. Omaha's odd 50-year-old example

Have a cup of coffee or three and get yourself a bicycle to explore the 120 miles of paved trails found across Omaha. Find them all at: https://parks.cityofomaha.org/parks/trails

*A look inside the Bike Union on Dodge Street.*

of futuristic architecture got a new lease on life in 2015 with the opening of the Bike Union and Coffee. Yes, the Bike Union sells coffee along with bicycles and has hosted an occasional poetry reading. The Bike Union also provides mentoring and an introduction to the workforce for teenagers aging out of Nebraska's foster care system.

## FUTURISM TODAY

**What:** A bicycle and coffee shop with a mission and unusual architecture

**Where:** 1818 Dodge St.

**Cost:** Free to visit during business hours

**Pro Tip:** In 2012, Omaha's Restoration Exchange sponsored a tour of Mid-Century Modern homes and businesses in the upscale Indian Hills neighborhood that was developed after 1958. Highlights of the tour can be found here: https://www. restorationexchange.org/ wp-content/uploads/2017/12/ Mid-Century-Modern-Tour-Brochure.pdf

# CUTLER'S PARK

## Can you organize wagons into a town?

Along an ordinary stretch of the Mormon Bridge Road once stood Nebraska's first organized city. Cutler's Park was just tents and wagons, but it was arranged into square blocks with a population of some 2,500 Mormons by early August 1846. There was a town square, a ban on public burning, 24 policemen and fireguards, and a fine line between civil and church government. The site was near a small tributary of Mill Creek and was discovered by (and named after) Alpheus Cutler, a high priest and member of Joseph Smith's exclusive Anointed Quorum who helped lead the Mormons from Nauvoo.

In late August 1846, residents were confronted by the actual owners of the land: the Omaha and the Otoe and Missouria. Rent was due where available resources were already stretched thin. Mormon leader Brigham Young and Omaha Chief Big Elk came to an agreement: the Mormons could remain if they'd move closer to the river. Promises of protection were likely made as well. Cutler's Park was gradually abandoned after just over a month in existence, as the Mormons moved a few miles northeast to Winter Quarters. Cutler's Park would be the end of the Mormon Trail for the dozens who died there, mostly in September and October.

## CITY OF WAGONS

**What:** Small memorial for a Mormon camp named after an apostate.

**Where:** Northeast corner of Mormon Bridge Rd. and Young St.

**Cost:** Free to visit during daylight hours

**Pro Tip:** There's a small marker on the northwest corner of S. 60th and L Sts. that describes the first Mormon camp west of the Missouri River. Cold Springs Camp was used very briefly in 1846 while Mormon leaders debated where to spend the winter.

*The Cutler's Park Memorial on North Mormon Bridge Road*

Cutler grew dissatisfied with Brigham Young's growing influence. He moved his followers to a new settlement on Silver Creek in Iowa and worked to establish a mission among the Native Americans in Kansas. They were disfellowshipped by the Mormons who were heading west to Salt Lake City, and instead, Cutler founded his own church and led his followers east.

Cutler led his followers to a settlement called Manti some 60 miles southeast of Omaha, where he died in 1864. The site of the former town is now a county park near Shenandoah, Iowa.

# RESTING PLACE OF THE OMAHA KID

## What more stories can you find?

St. Mary's Cemetery is the oldest of Omaha's Catholic cemeteries; the first Catholic burial took place there in 1883. The cemetery contains some interesting and solemn religious ornamentation along with a wealth of old South Omaha names and stories. There's Mary Kilker, who was 87 years old when she died in 1916. She had immigrated from Ireland in 1856 and arrived in Omaha that year onboard a Missouri River steamboat. There are cousins Mary Sheehan and Mary Looney, who both drowned in Lake Manawa in 1906. There was an honor guard at the 1922 burial of 28-year-old Lester Southwick. Southwick was the first Omahan drafted into WWI.

This cemetery is also the final resting place of Jack Lawler, the boxer sometimes promoted as the "Omaha Kid," who might have been somebody. His first fight was in 1917. In September 1918, Lawler fought Billy Schauers, called by the *Bee* the "Light Weight Champion of the Army" at an Omaha Elks and Salvation Army exhibition. At New Orleans, Lawler defeated Phil Virgets in 15 rounds in November 1919 and knocked out Red Dolan after seven rounds in December 1920. In January 1922, Lawler's mother had a ringside seat to watch her son beat Johnny Noye in 10 rounds at Omaha. The next month, he was billed as a "junior lightweight championship" contender by the *Bee* in Tulsa, where he outpointed Gene Delmont after 12 rounds.

Two recipients of the Congressional Medal of Honor are buried at St. Mary's: Patrick F. Ford, Jr. and Edward "Babe" Gomez.

*Some of the elaborate memorial stones at St. Mary's Cemetery*

Whatever might have been, in June 1924 there was either a bungled hold-up or a drunken mix-up at a South Omaha restaurant, and Jack Lawler was shot dead by Omaha police officer M. F. Nielson.

## SO MANY STORIES IN STONES

**What:** A historic cemetery

**Where:** 3353 Q St.

**Cost:** Free to visit during daylight hours

**Pro Tip:** Definitely stop next door at the Lithuanian Bakery at 5217 S. 33rd St. It was opened in 1962 by Lithuanian immigrants Vytautas and Stefanija Mackevicius. The Lithuanian immigrant mural decorates one side of the building that's home to rye bread, the world's best Napoleon Torte, and more.

# THE BYRON REED NUMISMATIC COLLECTION

## Do you want to see the money?

There's a lot to see around Omaha and even some old stuff by Midwestern standards. Still, what's the oldest? It might just be an ancient coin from the time of Julius Caesar. There's also a 1634 King James Bible and a letter from Catherine de Medici. The Byron Reed Numismatic Collection at the Durham Museum houses these artifacts along with Colonial and Confederate coins, an 1804 US silver dollar, a complete collection of American coins from 1792 through the 1890s, and other rarities that attract serious coin collectors from everywhere.

Byron Reed was born in Genesee County, New York, and became a telegraph operator after his family moved to Wisconsin. He went to Leavenworth, Kansas, in late 1855 as a correspondent for the *New York Tribune* until he was run out of town for anti-slavery sympathies. Reed went to Omaha and opened a real estate office in 1856 that made him very wealthy. He was also elected Omaha city clerk and later served on the city council. Reed was well known for his collection, considered by Alfred Sorenson as

## A COLLECTOR'S COLLECTION

**What:** Unique collection of coins and ephemera

**Where:** Lower level of the Durham Museum at 801 S. 10th St.

**Cost:** Please see www. durhammuseum.org for current admission and hours.

**Pro Tip:** The Durham is inside Omaha's 1931 Art Deco Union Station, where 10,000 people passed through daily in 1946. The Union Pacific donated the building to Omaha in 1973.

*The Byron Reed Collection is housed at the Durham Museum inside the 1931 Omaha Union Station on South 10th Street.*

"one of the most complete in the country" in 1888. When he died in 1891, Reed donated his coins, money, books, and everything else to the city of Omaha. Byron Reed's treasures were housed in a special room at the city's old library for years. In 1996, the city put some of the horde up for auction at Christie's and made $6.1 million. Only a portion of the remaining collection is on permanent display, tucked away in the lower level of the Durham Museum.

There have been occasional 'behind the scenes' tours in recent years that might offer a glimpse of something more.

The Byron Reed Collection was named one of the four money museums "every numismatist must visit" in 2018 by www.preferredcoinexchange.com.

# MR. BLANDINGS'S DREAM HOME

## Why did Hollywood build identical homes across the country?

There's a zany Hollywood promotion standing in plain sight in the middle of Omaha that seemed to almost encapsulate all of America's post-WWII desires. The book *Mr. Blandings Builds His Dream House* was published in 1946 and was based on author Eric Hodgins's own experiences. There seemed something very real about the premise to Americans trying to start a new life after victory in the war. The movie came out in 1948 and starred Cary Grant, Myrna Loy, and Melvyn Douglas. It was a romantic comedy that told the story of the Blandingses as they abandoned their cramped New York City apartment in favor of the Connecticut countryside. Their dream home desires soon turn into a laughable money pit of misadventures that found an easy audience as the suburbs started to spread.

Movie promotions included dollhouse plans included with Kellogg's cereal and "Dream Houses" identical to Mr. Blandings's home constructed across the country, including one in Omaha.

## HOLLYWOOD HOME IN OMAHA

**What:** 1948 home from a Hollywood movie

**Where:** 502 N. 72nd Ave.

**Cost:** Free to view during daylight hours

**Pro Tip:** Some real homes of Hollywood stars can also be found in Omaha, including 3135 Mason St. where Marlon Brando lived as a baby. Brando was born in Omaha in 1924 and later lived at 1026 S. 32nd St. In Omaha, Brando's mother Dodie encouraged young Henry Fonda's acting career. The Brandos moved to Illinois when Marlon was 11. He would win two academy awards for acting but turned one of them down.

*Mr. Blandings's Dream House in 2020.*

The tidy two-story Colonial was located in the new Underwood Hills housing development. Some 35,000 people went to see the new home with such luxuries as an all-electric kitchen with an automatic washing machine. The house was raffled off, with about 30,000 people purchasing a one-dollar raffle ticket. The dream home was won by Mr. and Mrs. Willey of Council Bluffs. They promptly sold it to an Omaha doctor and his wife, who raised six children there. The home was renovated in 2018.

RKO Pictures built 73 identical "Dream Houses" around the country to promote the movie.

# THE SINGING TOWER OF WESTLAWN

## How can a tower sing?

Unlike some pioneer burying grounds later engulfed by the city, Westlawn was a planned enterprise, with the first 10 acres laid out in 1906 on the city's western edge. The city kept moving west while the cemetery (now known officially as Westlawn-Hillcrest) remains a peaceful retreat of 168 acres.

In its early years, Westlawn advertised its "convenient and modern park plan," "family lots on easy payments," and the "perpetual care" lacking in earlier cemeteries. They also advertised the convenience of an electric streetcar right to the front entrance while a telephone call would send out an automobile for those who needed to find a plot as fast as possible.

Westlawn has some interesting features, including a massive mausoleum built in 1915. The building measures fully 82 by 145 feet and was built "Doric in style" out of Colorado-Yule marble with 650 crypts and a columbarium. One 1915 advertisement called it a "beautiful white marble temple," and it does seem like it was plucked right out of Ancient Greece and placed atop a hill in Nebraska. There's also a Spanish-American War memorial

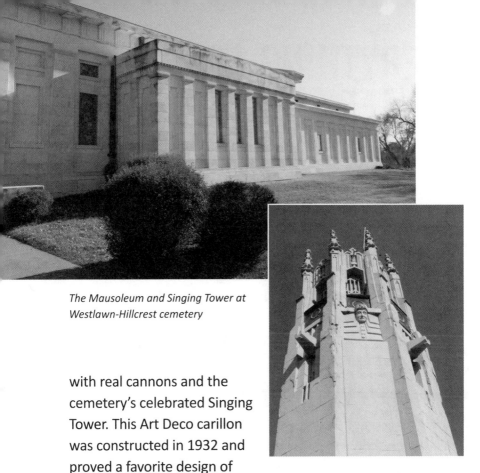

*The Mausoleum and Singing Tower at Westlawn-Hillcrest cemetery*

with real cannons and the cemetery's celebrated Singing Tower. This Art Deco carillon was constructed in 1932 and proved a favorite design of Omaha architect Fred A. Henninger, Jr. The Singing Tower is in the Hillcrest section dominated by flat stones. At one time, there was a studio with an organ inside for vocal and instrumental performances that brought crowds just to listen. Much of what once made the tower sing has now gone silent, although recorded music is still played.

The president of Westlawn was N.P. Dodge II, who moved his family's well known real estate business from Council Bluffs to Omaha in 1900.

# EVERYTHING AT THE CENTER

## Who brought the shopping mall to Omaha?

The mid-20th century development of the enclosed shopping mall was a marvel of rebranding ingenuity. The new shopping malls had everything that used to be found on a small-town Main Street or at any of the big-city downtown department stores. Everything was available in a single, climate-controlled environment, no matter the weather outside, with convenient parking. The whole idea of shopping would be transformed, and one of America's first shopping malls was The Center Mall right at South 42nd and Center Streets.

Groundbreaking for the 195,000-square-foot shopping facility took place in August 1954. The new shopping center planned to house 30 stores with parking for 1,000 automobiles. Unlike when shopping downtown, no one needed to pay any parking meters. The Center opened in September 1955 with the Des Moines department store chain Younkers as an original tenant. Early businesses included a Shavers supermarket, a cocktail lounge, and a camera shop, along with the mall's upstairs Sky Lanes bowling alley and Sky Room restaurant. At the official October dedication, the nine-year-old daughter of John Wiebe, the Center's builder, placed a time capsule on the site, which was supposed to be opened in 2005. There is

A Cinnabon store at an Omaha mall is one setting for the AMC television series *Better Call Saul*, but the nearest one to The Center is in a strip mall at 3605 Summit Plaza Dr. in Bellevue.

*A look inside the Center in 2020*

no record if it ever was opened, or what happened to it. The Center's architect predicted in the *Nonpareil* newspaper that by the time the capsule was opened the shopping mall would be a "bus stop for helicopters," while area resident Kenneth C. Welch believed the place would have to make room for "atomic-powered automobiles." Today, many Old English elements remain from the mall's remodeling following a 1969 fire.

## OMAHA'S FIRST MALL

**What:** An early shopping mall converted to offices

**Where:** 1941 S. 42nd St.

**Cost:** Free to visit during daylight hours

**Pro Tip:** Nebraska's largest shopping mall, with over a million square feet of retail space, is the still-busy Westroads at 10000 California St. Westroads first opened in 1967 and was also designed and developed by John Wiebe.

# LAST HOME OF THE TONG

## Where was Chinatown?

There are still branches of the On Leong Tong Chinese Merchants Association today, but their Omaha operations ended rather quietly in 1959. No one is certain when the tong first originated in the city. The first Chinese immigrants arrived in Omaha after the completion of the transcontinental railroad, although never in large numbers, and they never seemed to stay long. During the early 20th century, the tongs dominated Chinese immigrant communities and had control over vice, illegal immigration, opium, and gambling. The On Leong Tong seemed to have control from Omaha east to New York City. It competed with the Hip Sing Tong based in Denver. The tong wars of the 1920s were a real thing when Omaha's tong was located at 111 North 12th Street.

The Great Depression brought an end to the small Chinatown around 12th and Dodge Streets. It was said that many Chinese left for Texas, and there is no trace of that neighborhood today. At the same time, several Chinese immigrants in Omaha had relocated near North 16th and Cass Streets. In 1938 the Omaha tong moved into the building that still stands on Cass Street. The tong house was divided between a gambling room and a Buddhist shrine as in its twilight years the tong members seemed to divide their time between mah-

Chinese immigrants from across the West met in Omaha in 1894 to organize a Geehing organization to overthrow the Manchurian Dynasty.

*The last home of the Omaha tong on Cass Street.*

## RELIC OF CHINATOWN

**What:** Last Omaha home of the On Leong Tong Chinese Merchant Association

**Where:** 1518 Cass St.

**Cost:** Free to view during daylight hours

**Pro Tip:** Until King Fong's at 315 S. 16th St. reopens, the best bet to find Chinese food downtown might be the Panda House at 301 S. 16th St., with its great windows for street watching.

jong and socializing. Omaha's branch of the On Leong Tong disbanded with the 1959 death of George Hay, one of its last members. The building was listed on the National Register of Historic Places in 2017.

# THE *TÄGLICHE OMAHA TRIBÜNE*

## How did the Germans in America get their news?

There was once a German-language newspaper empire based out of Omaha. Valentin Peter was born in the small Bavarian village Steinbach am Wald, but he was named a papal Knight of St. Gregory before he died in 1960. He was 14 years old in 1889 when he immigrated with his parents and two sisters to Rock Island, Illinois. Ten years later, he took over Rock Island's German-language newspaper and ran it for eight years before moving to Omaha. He soon set about consolidating the city's various German newspapers and, in 1912, started publication of the *Tägliche Omaha Tribüne*, a weekly that grew into a major voice for German immigrants. Peter continued to expand and took over a string of German newspapers, first across Nebraska and Iowa and then from Colorado to Chicago and Buffalo.

Peter was president of the German Alliance of Nebraska as World War I approached, and everything changed. In November 1915, he joined with Mayor Dahlman and hundreds of others at Omaha's German Musikverein to benefit war relief. By April 1918, the *Bee* newspaper reported Peter was "keeping alive the good old German language" as new laws ended instruction in schools. At the same time, if the "language and customs of the Fatherland were to be perpetuated" Peter badly needed money, so he asked readers to subscribe for two years in advance so that he could "keep alive all he can of Germany in America."

Valentin Peter was named Nebraska's representative for the German and Austrian consulate in 1922.

*The former home of the Tribüne on Howard Street is now part of the J.P. Cooke complex*

A week after his subscription request, Peter was subject to investigation following a motion by Gage County, Nebraska's Council of Defense for what the *Bee* called the "suppression" of the Omaha newspaper. The *Tägliche Omaha Tribüne* ceased publication in 1926.

## HISTORIC BUSINESS ON HOWARD STREET

**What:** Site of an influential German language newspaper

**Where:** 1311 Howard St. is now occupied by J.P. Cooke, a manufacturer in business in Omaha since 1887.

**Cost:** Free to view during daylight hours.

**Pro Tip:** Thanks to a $200,000 grant to the University of Nebraska at Lincoln, most issues of The *Tägliche Omaha Tribüne* have been digitized and are now available to the public through the Library of Congress at https://chroniclingamerica.loc.gov.

# GIBSON

## How does a community start in boxcars?

Omaha has the reputation as a Union Pacific town, but there's another place almost hidden away at the bottom of the bluffs along the Missouri River. These are the BNSF rail yards at Gibson Bend, and they don't draw much attention. There's also an intermodal transfer facility at what used to be the Burlington railroad's Gibson Station. The grain elevator, coal chutes, roundhouse, and turntable are all gone, but there are still trains and an atypical history.

The Missouri River gives up its dead at Gibson Bend. In March 1901, the body of a young woman was discovered still frozen in the sand at Gibson. She'd been missing for four months. That October, three 12-year-old boys found the body of a boy their own age in the river near Gibson. All he had was a loaded .22 revolver, a tobacco sack, and a pencil. There were more. The railroad yards could also be deadly, and in January 1904, Burlington railroad worker C. G. Hedburg was killed by the No. 4 passenger train here.

The railroad brought all sorts, and in May 1913 Gibson was "swarming with hoboes." In 1922, the yards were guarded by Omaha police during a railroad strike. The railroad also brought a colonia as one of Omaha's first Mexican-immigrant neighborhoods. Revolutions brought growing numbers of immigrants with 50 families and likely more single men, mostly

---

Today, almost 14 percent of Omaha is Hispanic, and El Museo Latino is located at 4701 South 25th Street.

*The view east to Gibson from South 1st and Hascall Streets.*

living in converted boxcars. By 1923, the Baptists were giving English lessons at what the *Bee* described as the "Mexican settlement at Gibson" and then started holding classes in a converted boxcar.

## RAILROAD HISTORY

**What:** A rail yard with a past

**Where:** 100 Hascall St.

**Cost:** Free to view during daylight hours, but stay off railroad property.

**Pro Tip:** The railroad at the Henry Doorly Zoo at 3701 S. 10th St. is a 1.8-mile narrow-gauge with two steam locomotives: the *119* (custom-built for the zoo in 1968) and the *Riva* (manufactured in Linz, Austria, in 1904).

# HOME OF AN ICE BARON

## How do you get rich off ice?

It seems we all take refrigeration for granted as air conditioning keeps everything the same steady temperature. Who hasn't had that package of peas in the back of the freezer forever? But simple ice was a serious commodity when meatpacking was a major industry. Omaha's annual ice harvest from the river and local lakes amounted to 125,000 tons in 1886. The *Bee* newspaper called that year's ice "good quality but not the best." All efforts had been made to avoid places "affected by the sewerage from the pipes." By 1916, Omaha's ice harvest employed up to 5,000 people.

John P. Bay was a co-founder of the Crystal Ice Company, and in 1887 Omaha architect George Fisher designed his Queen Anne mansion. The home's striking S-shaped tower has dominated North 21st and Binney Streets. for over 130 years. In 1887 the Kountze Place neighborhood was annexed by Omaha as a comfortable suburb convenient to downtown via the streetcars. In 1889, the Crystal Ice Company

---

## HISTORIC HOME

**What:** The mansion of an ice baron

**Where:** 2024 Binney St.

**Cost:** Free to view during daylight hours

**Pro Tip:** Some other interesting Kountze Place properties of note include the 1903 George F. Shepherd home at 1802 Wirt St., the 1909 Charles Stortz home at 1901 Wirt St., and the 1918 George H. Kelly House at 1924 Binney St.

---

The John P. Bay/Thomas A. Fry Home was named an Omaha Landmark in 1981.

*The 1887 mansion of John Bay on Binney Street.*

had 300 men out cutting ice on the river and Carter Lake. According to the *Bee*, the ice was "very clear but only about ten inches thick."

The Binney Street home was later owned by Thomas A. Fry. Fry had a shoe store at 1415 Douglas Street in 1894 but is better remembered as a founder of Omaha's Knights of Ak-Sar-Ben in 1895. Fry was one of the original members of the board of directors and served as president in 1902. He was also a member of Omaha's Board of Education.

# DRUID HALL

## Who are the Prince Hall Masons?

There's a strikingly Gothic structure along Ames Avenue just west of North 24th Street. It was designed by German immigrant Joseph P. Guth. Guth worked as an architect in Germany before he immigrated in 1884 and worked as a civil engineer for railroads in Ohio and Minnesota. He started in Omaha working for the Union Pacific railroad before returning to architecture. The *Bee* newspaper called the building a "Palatial Temple" when it opened in 1915 as the home for the Woodman of the World Druid Camp #24, a fraternal organization with insurance benefits. At the time they had 800 members and they'd worked for nine years to make the new building a reality. There was a hardware store on the first floor along with various meeting rooms and a kitchen, and the second floor became known for its dances. There was a library, gymnasium, six pool tables, showers, and two bowling alleys in the basement.

In 1935, The D. Louis Black Post 3421 of the Veterans of Foreign Wars moved into Druid Hall. In December 1937, the *Guide* newspaper noted the "negro orchestra" played there as part of the Work Progress Administration's Federal Music Project, and the upstairs dances at Druid Hall continued into the 1950s. Since 1968 the building has been home to the Most Worshipful Prince Hall Grand Lodge of Nebraska. These "Prince Hall Masons" are America's oldest African-American fraternal organization and originated after Boston freemasons refused

Druid Hall was listed on the National Register of Historic Places in 2015.

*Druid Hall on Ames Avenue in 2020.*

to recognize 14 men as members because of the color of their skin. Instead, they would gain official recognition from the British Masons and first organized in Omaha in the 1870s.

## HISTORIC HALL

**What:** A historic fraternal hall and community center

**Where:** 2412 Ames Ave.

**Cost:** Free to view during daylight hours

**Pro Tip:** A truly spectacular Masonic building in the city is the Scottish Rite Cathedral at 202 S. 20th St. The building opened in 1914 and is still home to the Scottish Rite.

# SITE OF THE ST. NICHOLAS

## Where was the first building in Omaha?

In July 1854, William and Rachel Snowden took a flatboat ferry across the Missouri River from Council Bluffs, Iowa. The ink was barely dry on the Kansas-Nebraska Act when the Snowdens became Omaha's first permanent white residents. The Snowden's first home, and the first home in the city, was a one-room cottonwood log structure with an attached kitchen. It was built by Tom Allen for the Council Bluffs & Nebraska Ferry Company at what became the southwest corner of South 12th and Jackson Streets. The Snowden's first home also served as a crude boarding house with accommodations on the floor or under your wagon outside. Omaha's first official church services were held there in August 1854 by a Methodist minister from Council Bluffs. This was officially named the St. Nicholas but was mostly called the "Claim House." The building was constructed to establish the ferry company's land claim, where they intended to create and promote a brand-new Nebraska city.

Omaha's second building was at North 22nd and Burt Streets, and the third was the "Big 6." The "Big 6" was a combination saloon and grocery store located in a sod "dug-

*Historic plaques adorn Hollywood Candy at South 12th and Jackson Streets*

HISTORIC BUILDING SITE

out" on the north side of Chicago between North 13th and 14th Streets. William Snowden then built the city's fourth building on the west side of South 10th Street. The lot had been given to the Snowdens on condition they build on it. After three months at the St. Nicholas, the Snowdens moved into their new home and celebrated with an all-night dance. A Mr. Leonard played the fiddle for the affair.

To promote their new city, the ferry company built Omaha's first brick building and gave it to the Nebraska Territory for use as a seat of government.

# THE LAST OF JOBBER'S CANYON

## What happened along the riverfront?

The 1906 building, now known as the Greenhouse Apartments, is another significant Omaha landmark designed by architect Thomas Kimball. This eight-story building was designed as a factory, and wholesale warehouse for M. E. Smith & Company and originally had a duplicate standing adjacent. M. E. Smith was a large wholesale dry goods firm with trade across the West all the way up to Alaska. In November 1905, the *Bee* reported Kimball accompanied a lawyer and the heads of M. E. Smith to examine "wholesale houses" in Kansas City and St. Louis. They also planned to go to Minneapolis, and construction in Omaha would naturally depend on the weather.

Today this building is the last remnant of Jobber's Canyon and seems somewhat a sore thumb from what used to be a unique wholesale and jobbing district near the Omaha riverfront. The Canyon was made up of massive wholesale warehouses connected by a tangle of railroad tracks to distribute goods from Omaha to all points of the country. It was located from Farnam south to Jackson Street and from South 10th Street west to South 13th Street. In 1979, 29 buildings in Jobber's Canyon were listed on the National Register of Historic Places. A decade later, all were razed except the Nash Block. That was followed

The razing of Jobber's Canyon was the largest delisting of properties from the National Register of Historic Places in American history.

*The Greenhouse Apartments on Farnam Street.*

by construction of a suburban-style office park as the corporate headquarters for ConAgra Foods. The company's corporate headquarters relocated to Chicago in 2015 and in 2020 work was underway to transform 23 acres into a mixed-use development called the Mercantile.

## OLD BRICK WAREHOUSE

**What:** A historic warehouse converted to apartments

**Where:** 900 Farnam St.

**Cost:** Free to view during daylight hours

**Pro Tip:** Just west of the Nash Block is Omaha's old Burlington & Missouri River railroad headquarters at 1004 Farnam St., and it's well worth a look inside during normal business hours. The building was originally constructed in 1879 and was redesigned by Thomas Kimball 20 years later with an interior skylight and other decorative features.

# OMAHA'S FIRST SKYSCRAPER

## What was the tallest building in town?

Every Midwestern city always points out its imposing skyline as a point of pride and a symbol of something more in a land otherwise dominated by wide open farm fields. Across most of Nebraska, that means those giant grain elevators down by the railroad tracks. In Omaha in 1889, the renowned New York architectural firm of McKim, Mead and White was hired by the New York Life Insurance Company, and Frederick Hill designed the city's first real skyscraper. Although Omaha's New York Life Insurance Company Building was only 10 stories tall, until 1890 the tallest building in America was the 10 story Chicago Board of Trade. This new building was surely something significant for Omaha and even has a twin down in Kansas City.

The new building offered 300 rooms and four passenger elevators that the *Bee* newspaper claimed would take "a man

The adjacent WoodmenLife Building at 1700 Farnam Street was where Jack Nicholson's title character had his office in the 2002 motion picture *About Schmidt*.

*Omaha's 10-story New York Life Insurance Company Building and adjacent 30-story WoodmenLife Tower.*

from cellar to dome in half a minute." There were also electric lights and steam heating. The building was sold to Omaha National Bank in 1910 and remained Omaha's tallest building until the 1912 completion of the since-razed W.O.W. Building at 1323 Farnam Street. Of particular note is the building's ornamental bronze eagle designed by artist Louis St. Gaudens. The eagle lost its perch in the late 1960s, and Omaha National Bank left in 1972. The razing of the building seemed likely until 1978, when it was purchased by the Kutak Rock law firm. In 1997, the eagle was restored to its former place of prominence four stories above Farnam Street.

# THE FARMERS HOME

## Where was Millard's only hotel?

Sometimes the real wealth from the Union Pacific Railroad came from more than hauling cattle and cowboys. In 1866 Ezra Millard became president of the new Omaha National Bank, and he was mayor of Omaha from 1869 until 1871. In 1873, he platted a new town called, appropriately enough, Millard. This new town was on the West Branch of Papillion Creek along the original Union Pacific railroad's oxbow route, which was created to grab more land and money during construction.

Ezra Millard died in 1886, and his namesake town could sometimes be a rough-and-tumble place. In 1886 Herman Mittman ran a Millard saloon, and the *Bee* newspaper reported "had some troubles" with a customer so "tried to shoot him." A bar patron named Walter Durham tried to make peace with all present when "Mittman fired at Durham and killed him." The charge against Mittman was reduced to manslaughter, but he absconded before he was due in court.

In 1901 the Farmers Home Hotel was constructed, and Millard was still a very small town. Eleven years later, the Farmers Home and owner C. Hans Seick were both named in a mandamus suit for violating the liquor laws. The Farmers Home was up for sale by 1914, when it was advertised in the *Bee* newspaper as the town's only hotel featuring "good automobile and transient trade." The 1958 opening of the Western Electric plant at 132nd and L Streets brought about the town's explosive

Millard Days is held annually in August at Andersen Park in celebration of the once independent town with a carnival, parade, horseshoe contest, music, and more.

*Olympia Cycle in the former Farmers Home Hotel on South 135th Street*

growth and ultimate annexation by Omaha. The old Western Electric plant closed in 2011, and the site has been redeveloped. The Farmers Home has been closed for a long time too, and the unusual building is now the home of Omaha's Olympic Cycles.

## AN OLD HOTEL

**What:** The 1901 Farmers Home Hotel

**Where:** 4910 S. 135 St.

**Cost:** Free to visit during normal business hours. Call 402-554-1940 or see olympiaycleomaha.com.

**Pro Tip:** To keep "Old Millard" alive, a giant lumberyard nearby was reconstituted into the Lumberyard District. There are apartments along with Local, Beer, Patio and Kitchen at 4909 S. 135 St., which offers 100 local beers on tap along with a worthwhile kitchen.

# A PARK FOR SURVIVORS

## What parks were established by a founder of H&R Block?

There's a blink-and-you'll-miss-it green spot amongst the parking lots along the south side of busy Pacific Street through the Regency neighborhood. It is a place intended for contemplation, understanding, healing, and hope. Sometimes, it is a place for mourning. This is Omaha's Richard and Annette Bloch Cancer Survivors Park. Bloch came from a Jewish family in Kansas City and provided the R for the business that he and his brother Henry named H&R Block in 1955. In 1978, Richard was diagnosed with cancer and told he had only a few months to live. He decided to fight, won, and began funding cancer research, and started the R. A. Bloch Cancer Foundation. In June 1986, the Foundation began hosting Cancer Survivors Day rallies, and in 1990 the first Cancer Survivors Park opened in Kansas City. According to Bloch, "People see the signs and they get the idea that cancer does not mean death. . . . When their cancer is diagnosed, they will remember the park, and think of those words and feel hope."

There are now Cancer Survivors Parks in cities around the country. Each one is specific to its own locality, but all share the essential message of recovery. Omaha's Cancer Survivors Park features an arboretum that leads to 14 stainless-steel columns meant to resemble a column of light. There are also sculptures

*Sculptures at Cancer Survivors Park along Pacific Street.*

illustrating the varied stages of a cancer patient. The sculptures *Cancer, There is Hope* were the final works completed by Mexican sculptor Victor Salmones. Richard Bloch died in 2004 at the age of 78 (of heart failure, not cancer), and his inspirational vision continues in Omaha and elsewhere.

Cancer Survivors Park is adjacent to the 9.88 mile Big Papio Trail.

# BIG ELK

## Why was his grave moved twice?

He was named *Ong-pa-tonga* and was born in the early 1770s, when Nebraska started to change fast and forever. In English, he was Big Elk and led the Omaha people during a time of traumatic transition. When he was young, the Omaha lived at *Ton-wa-tonga* in Dakota County, Nebraska. At that time, Chief Blackbird controlled the flow of goods along the Missouri River no matter what gifts the fur traders brought from Spanish St. Louis.

Big Elk was forced to face both smallpox and war as Omaha interests were disrupted and then overrun by American influence and expansion. The Omaha were first forced from their summer hunting grounds on the Platte River and by 1820 relocated south to the Elkhorn River. The next year, two of Big Elk's brothers were killed fighting Sioux near Fort Atkinson. The Omaha would move again and relocate closer to Bellevue. After a visit to Washington, Big Elk warned the Omaha of a "coming flood" that would erase everything and "it will be very hard for you." He advised, "Speak kindly to one another; do what you can to help each other, even in the troubles with the coming tide." He died in 1848 and was buried west of Bellevue's Presbyterian Mission. In March 1854, Omaha

## BIG ELK'S BURIAL SPOT

**What:** Gravesite of an Omaha Chief

**Where:** The entrance to Bellevue cemetery is at W. 13th Ave. and Franklin St.

**Cost:** Free to visit during daylight hours

**Pro Tip:** The Bellevue cemetery was established in 1856. It is likely older and is still active, with a variety of monuments from the past 160 or so years. Perhaps one of the most poignant is a stone cairn that marks the undated grave of an unknown pioneer child buried while passing through at what is only described as an "early date."

*The gravestone for Big Elk in Bellevue.*

leaders signed the treaty that established the present Omaha Reservation with tribal headquarters at Macy, Nebraska.

Big Elk's burial site was disturbed during the 1883 construction of old Bellevue College, and his remains were reburied near Clark Hall. In 1954, the remains of Big Elk and other presumed Omaha were moved a third time to the Bellevue cemetery. There's a nice bench there to sit and think.

Big Elk's original burial place, called Onpontonga Xiathon, was near 400 West 19th Avenue in Bellevue.

# HELL'S HALF ACRE

## How did Omaha get a reputation?

There was a semi-legal section of sin that thrived for decades in Omaha. During the 1880s, the city gained electric lights, streetcars, and telephones, while part of town remained right out of the Wild West. The *Bee* newspaper called Omaha's red-light district "Hell's Half Acre," and its reputation as a place to lose your innocence, money, or life was well-earned. The vice district grew west of the Missouri River steamboat landing and Union Pacific shop yards, where brothels and gambling dens freely operated as long as they paid their monthly fines to the city. The point of Omaha's vice laws was not to stop crime, but instead to provide an easy stream of badly needed municipal revenue without raising anyone's taxes. The system dated from the city's earliest days and was rife with expected kick-backs and corruption. In Omaha's red light district, the rent was high, work was hard, and future prospects varied and unknown for the many women who worked there.

## THE WILD SIDE OF TOWN

**What:** Omaha's historic red light district.

**Where:** Douglas St. north to Capitol Ave. from 9th St. west to 15th St.

**Cost:** Free to visit with metered parking

**Pro Tip:** You can walk around with a beer at the new Capitol District entertainment area. For those who want a more intimate encounter around Omaha's red light district, please see the Wicked Omaha tour at http://historywalksnebraska.com/

There were 2,500 women living in Omaha's red light district in 1911.

*The last historic buildings on the north side of Douglas Street.*

Anna Wilson's high-toned brothel at 912 Douglas Street would have seemed stately in Omaha's most exclusive neighborhoods. There were cribs along Capitol Avenue, and the four-story Castle was at 9th and Dodge Streets. The entrance to The Arcade was at 912 Dodge Street with 200 women available in a block-long alley lit with electricity and dominated by large windows for easy advertising. In 1911, Nebraska passed the Albert Law, which ended the restricted district and instead just spread vice throughout downtown.

# DUNDEE STREETCARS

## Where in Omaha couldn't you get a beer?

Dundee was intended to be a place outside the city but still connected to it, and remains one of Omaha's best examples of a streetcar suburb. Appropriately, there's an interesting monument dedicated to Dundee streetcars not far from the end of the line. In July 1887, 50 men and 32 teams of horses were grading the new 1 1/2-mile-long Underwood Avenue through John Patrick's "Happy Hollow" farm. This was Dundee Place, named after a recent Kansas City project, and the Patrick Land Company advertised in the *Bee* newspaper in August the "gently rolling" lots for sale and promised that the "Cable Road" would be completed there within 18 months. Advertisements in the *Bee* newspaper from September 1889 noted that Dundee Place was "restricted against nuisances" with saloons forbidden.

Dundee Place finally got streetcars in June 1891, when the Metropolitan Cable Railway started with horse-drawn streetcars. The route ran from a connection with the Omaha Street Railway at South 40th and Farnam Streets and followed Underwood Avenue from North 49th Street to the western terminus at North 52nd Street. Rides were free at first as a wonderful way to promote the new

---

### STREETCAR MEMORIAL

**What:** A monument to Dundee's streetcars

**Where:** Southwest corner of Underwood Ave. and Happy Hollow Blvd.

**Cost:** Free to visit during daylight hours

**Pro Tip:** Dundee's Community Garden was established in 2009 at 4902 Underwood Ave. to provide the neighborhood with fresh local produce. See https://www.dundeegarden.org/ for the variety of events and workshops also hosted there.

*The memorial to Dundee streetcars at Underwood Avenue and Happy Hollow Boulevard*

development. The streetcar went electric in 1892 and bumped fares up to a nickel.

The lots did not sell, and instead, Dundee was incorporated as its own village in 1894. The Metropolitan Cable Railway became part of the Omaha & Council Bluffs Street Railway in 1902. Dundee real estate did not take off until after 1905. Dundee was annexed by Omaha in 1915, and the last streetcar ran down Underwood Avenue in March 1955.

The residential neighborhood north and west of nearby Memorial Park was dubbed Bagel due the large number of Jewish residents.

# AROUND THE WORLD TO OMAHA

## Who put the Train in Traintown?

It's likely George Francis Train provided some inspiration for the character of Phileas Fogg in Jules Verne's novel *Around the World in 80 Days*. Misadventures of fictional Englishmen hardly compare to "America's Champion Crank." The newspapers called this eccentric visionary and smooth-talking businessman the "greatest of American bombasts," "lunatic," and "political clown." He supported feminists, Fenians, and French Communards, and he built England's first street railways. Train ran for President and received no votes, was jailed twice in Europe, and convinced the Queen of Spain to finance a Pennsylvania railroad.

He first got rich off transit lines between Australia and England and then during the Gold Rush. Train was instrumental in developing the Union Pacific Railroad and Omaha with it. His brother-in-law was Dr. Thomas Durant, and Train first came up with Crédit Mobilier and associated Credit Foncier real estate company to make fortunes building the transcontinental railroad. He spoke at the Union Pacific's 1863 Omaha groundbreaking and developed "Train

## HISTORIC SCHOOL

**What:** An old school in Train Town

**Where:** 1615 S. 6th St.

**Cost:** Free to view during daylight hours

**Pro Tip:** George Bemis worked to develop the Bemis Park neighborhood platted in 1889 with streets that followed the lay of the land instead of the city grid. The 1913 Easter tornado devastated the neighborhood, which was listed as an Omaha Landmark in 1983. The Zabriskie House at 3524 Hawthorne Ave. and Porter-Thomsen House at 3426 Lincoln Blvd. are two notable residential homes in the neighborhood.

*The Train Town school is now home to the Alpha School.*

Town" south of the Missouri River railroad bridge. In 1871, Train set out on his first widely reported trip around the world. He did it again in 1890 in 67 days and in 1892 in 60 days. The "Train Town" school has long been at the same location, with the present building opening in 1894. Train ended up in New York City's Madison Park giving out dimes to children until his 1905 death.

For many of his adventures, Train was accompanied by his nephew George Bemis as a potential Jean Passepartout. Bemis came to Omaha as part of Credit Foncier, stayed for good, and served as mayor from 1892 until 1896.

George Francis Train's Omaha home was located at South 7th and Pine Streets, now the location of the pleasant Dahlman Park at 615 Pine Street.

# SOURCES

**Omaha Blues**
https://www.wirz.de/music/willbigj.htm http://msbluestrail.org/blues-trail-markers/big-joe-williams https://en.wikipedia.org/wiki/Big_Joe_Williams; https://northomahahistory.com/2016/07/08/a-short-history-of-the-24th-and-lake-historic-district-in-north-omaha-nebraska/ https://www.nps.gov/nr/feature/places/pdfs/16000159. pdf; https://gpblackhistorymuseum.org/

**Little Italy's Giant Fork**
*Omaha World-Herald*. "Check out Little Italy's giant fork" May 24, 2019. https://www.omaha.com/check-out-little-italys-giant-fork/image_9ed0289c-7c5a-5abe-a693-b9 ef 9ed51ed8.html; http://jakebalcomsculpture.com/work#/new-gallery-3/; *Omaha Magazine*. "Little Italy, Big Flavor" August 12, 2014.; "Opportunity attracted thousands of Italians to Early Omaha" David Harding. *Omaha-World Herald* October 26, 2016.; https://en.wikipedia.org/wiki/Little_Italy,_Omaha https://orsibakery.com/

**Site of the Civic**
https://en.wikipedia.org/wiki/Omaha_Civic_Auditorium; http://www.gendisasters.com/nebraska/6345/omaha-ne-famous-circus-performer-killed-apr-1963; https://www.concertarchives.org/venues/omaha-civic-auditorium; *Omaha World-Herald* "The night George Wallace came to Omaha, and the night the 1968 race riot began." March 6, 2018. "Timeline: Civic Auditorium and Music Hall." March 20, 2018. https://en.wikipedia.org/wiki/CHI_Health_Center_Omaha

**A Garden with the Zodiac**
https://gardenofthezodiacgallery.com/history.html; *Lincoln Journal Star*. "The Mercer Family and Omaha's Old Market" June 25, 2016. *Omaha Magazine*. "Public Art Primer." June 20, 2013.

**An Explosion over Dundee**
https://www.npr.org/sections/npr-history-dept/2015/01/20/375820191/beware-of-japanese-balloon-bombs; *Omaha Magazine*. "Bombs bursting in air." September 14, 2014. https://www.visitomaha.com/things-to-do/entertaining-neighborhoods/dundee/

**Millard Sky Park**
*Omaha World-Herald*. "Millard may get its own jet soon." October 15, 1967. https://en.wikipedia.org/wiki/Millard_Airport_(Nebraska)

**The Omaha Platform**
https://northomahahistory.com/2017/05/11/aksarben/; https://web-clear.unt.edu/course_projects/HIST2610/content/05_Unit_Five/18_lesson_eighteen/ 09_pplst_prty.htm; https://en.wikipedia.org/wiki/People%27s_Party_(United_States)

**Get Scalped and Survive**
https://www.atlasobscura.com/places/william-thompson-s-scalped-scalp; https://omahalibrary.org/blogs/post/about-william-thompson-his-scalp/; https://www.wowt.com/2020/08/07/william-thompsons-153-year-old-scalp/

**The Best View of Omaha**
https://www.councilbluffs-ia.gov/2307/Lincoln-Monument ; https://www.atlasobscura.com/places/lincoln-monument-council-bluffs; https://culturenow.org/entry&permalink=11614&seo=Ruth-Anne-Dodge-Memorial_Daniel-Chester-French-and-Council-Bluffs-Parks-Recreation-and-Public-Property-Department; https://graveyardsofomaha.com/fairview/fairview_1.html

**Alone in the Missouri**
https://www.iowawestfoundation.org/initiatives/iowa-west-public-art/; Orr, Richard. *O&CB: Streetcars of Omaha and Council Bluffs*. Richard Orr, 1996. https://en.wikipedia.org/wiki/Ak-Sar-Ben_Bridge

**Aristotle in Omaha**
https://en.wikipedia.org/wiki/Omaha_Public_Library_(building); http://www.e-nebraskahistory.org/index.php?title=Thomas_Rogers_Kimball_(1862-1934),_Architect; https://en.wikipedia.org/wiki/Omaha_Public_Library_(building); https://sah-archipedia.org/buildings/NE-01-055-0006

**The Statue Saved from a Ditch**
*Omaha Daily Bee*. "Schiller Day in Omaha" July 15, 1907.; "Von Schiller, German poet, is given a coating of yellow." July 1, 1918.; *Omaha World-Herald*. "From the Archives: The Zoo" September 18, 2012. https://en.wikipedia.org/wiki/Friedrich_Schiller; https://www.germanamericansociety.org/

**A Memorial to Central Elementary**
*Omaha Daily Bee*."Opening of the schools." September 12, 1893.; https://en.wikipedia.org/wiki/Omaha_Central_High_School ; https://en.wikipedia.org/wiki/Northern_Natural_Gas_Building

**Benson and its Bunnies**
Orr, Richard. *O&CB: Streetcars of Omaha and Council Bluffs*. Richard Orr, 1996.; *Lincoln Journal Star*. "Benson: from Erastus A. Benson to the Benson Bunnies" August 26, 2012.; https://en.wikipedia.org/wiki/Omaha_Benson_High_School_Magnet

**Rosenfield's Peonies**
https://americanpeonysociety.org/cultivars/peony-registry/karl-rosenfield/; *Omaha World-Herald*. "Joe Malec just grew a peony!" August 18, 1968. https://en.wikipedia.org/wiki/Peony_Park

**The Bloody Corner**
*Omaha Daily Bee*. "Slayer of Serb is acquitted by jury." May 6, 1917. "Man killed by assassin, coroner's jury decides." June 3, 1922.; *Omaha World-Herald* "Plan in the works to tear-down Southside Terrace public housing apartments, redevelop site." May 29, 2016.

**Omaha's "Prettiest Mile"**
https://northomahahistory.com/2013/09/23/a-history-of-omahas-florence-boulevard/; https://northomahahistory.com/2016/11/03/broadview-hotel/; https://en.wikipedia.org/wiki/Horace_Cleveland; https://en.wikipedia.org/wiki/Boulevards_in_Omaha,_Nebraska

**Preserving Some Prairie**
https://www.unomaha.edu/college-of-arts-and-sciences/nature-preserves/preserves/index.php; https://www.unomaha.edu/news/2014/11/homepage/tbt-nov20.php; *Lincoln Journal Star*. "Glacier Creek protects prairie habitat" July 13, 2014.

**A Roller Coaster Disaster**
*Omaha Daily Bee*. "Tietz Park on the Military Road" June 30, 1885.; http://www.gendisasters.com/nebraska/13295/omaha-ne-amusement-park-accident-july-1930 *Omaha Magazine*. "Krug Park" April 28, 2015.; https://en.wikipedia.org/wiki/Frederick_Krug

**John O'Neill, the Hero of Ridgeway**
*Omaha Daily Bee*. "De Valera has busy day as Omaha Guest." October 29, 1919. https://en.wikipedia.org/wiki/John_O%27Neill_(Fenian); https://en.wikipedia.org/wiki/Battle_of_Ridgeway; http://graveyardsofomaha.com/holy_sepulchre/holysepulchre_main.html

**A Painting Attacked Twice**
https://en.wikipedia.org/wiki/William-Adolphe_Bouguereau; *Omaha World-Herald*. "Opening of Joslyn helped pave the way for 'Spring' to shine again. October 25, 2020. https://en.wikipedia.org/wiki/George_W._Lininger ; https://en.wikipedia.org/wiki/The_Return_of_Spring

**Who Killed Harry Lapidus**
Menard, Orville. *River City Empire: Tom Dennison's Omaha*. University of Nebraska Press, 1989.; *Omaha World-Herald*. "1931 slaying of businessman Harry Lapidus helped pry Omaha from mob's clutches" March 9, 2015.; https://en.wikipedia.org/wiki/Hanscom_Park

**Beadles Rock Brook Claim**
Beadle, Erastus. *Ham, Eggs, & Corn Cake: A Nebraska Territory Diary*. University of Nebraska Press, 2001.; https://en.wikipedia.org/wiki/Erastus_Flavel_Beadle; https://greatruns. com/omaha-ne-big-papio-trail/; https://www.ulib.niu.edu/badndp/dn-a.html; http:// douglascohistory.net/Education_Mayors_2.htm https://northomahahistory.com/2012/01/09/a-history-of-omahas-saratoga-neighborhood-aka-s ul phur-springs/

**Minne Lusa**
https://en.wikipedia.org/wiki/Minne_Lusa; https://northomahahistory.com/2016/06/24/a-history-of-the-minne-lusa-historic-district-in-north- omaha-nebraska/

**Some Copenhagen in Omaha**
Otis, Harry B., with Donald H. Erickson. *E Pluribus Omaha: Immigrants All*. Lamplighter Press, 2000.; *Omaha World-Herald*. "Only 50 years old, midtown's Danish Brotherhood building makes National Register of Historic Places" October 31, 2016.; "Documentary will highlight stories of early Danish immigrants in Nebraska, western Iowa" April 11, 2017.; https://en.wikipedia.org/ wiki/Danish_Brotherhood_in_America ; https://www.nps.gov/nr/feature/places/16000480. htm; https://en.wikipedia.org/wiki/Danish_people_in_Omaha,_Nebraska; https:// northomahahistory.com/2017/04/15/a-history-of-the-danish-vennelyst-park-in-north-oma h a/; https://www.danishvennelystpark.org/

**The Elmwood Grotto**
https://parks.cityofomaha.org/parks; *Omaha Magazine*. "Elmwood Park Paved for a Parking Lot" February 13, 2019.; *Omaha Daily Bee*. "West Siders Have a Grievance" July 7, 1896. September 18, 1918. June 29, 1919.

**The Murder at the University of Omaha**
*The Gateway*. "Police Search Continues for Carolyn Nevins' Slayer" December 16, 1955. "Murder of UNO student still unsolved 47 years later" October 29, 2002.; https://www.unomaha. edu/about-uno/buildings-and-maps/arts-and-sciences-hall.php; https://northomahahistory. com/2015/08/02/a-history-of-north-omahas-omaha-university-campu s/; https://www. unomaha.edu/about-uno/city-of-omaha.php#history; https://en.wikipedia.org/wiki/ December_1955; https://en.wikipedia.org/wiki/Redick_Mansion

**Sheelytown**
*Lincoln Journal Star* "Sheelytown almost but never quite an actual town" September 1, 2013. *Omaha Magazine*. "Sheelytown" October 10, 2016.; https://en.wikipedia.org/wiki/Sheelytown_ (Omaha)

**Walk with Standing Bear**
https://en.wikipedia.org/wiki/Standing_Bear_Lake; https://en.wikipedia.org/wiki/Standing_ Bear; *Omaha World-Herald* "Floating trail to open later this summer at Standing Bear Lake" May 29, 2020.; https://www.unomaha.edu/news/2017/08/river-runs-around-it.php; http://www. ohranger.com/standing-bear-lake

**That Florence Bank**
*Bellevue Gazette* January 28, 1858. March 11, 1858.; https://northomahahistory. com/2018/05/18/a-history-of-the-north-side-bank/ ; https://en.wikipedia.org/wiki/Bank_of_ Florence_Museum ; http://www.historicflorence.org/Attractions/bank.php; *Omaha World-Herald*. "In North Omaha's Florence neighborhood...buildings from the 1800s have been preserved" February 26, 2017.; http://sarpycountymuseum.org/2016/08/the-fontenelle-bank/

**Union Pacific Shop Yards Monument**

https://en.wikipedia.org/wiki/Union_Pacific_Railroad_Omaha_Shops_Facility ; https://en.wikipedia.org/wiki/McKeen_Motor_Car_Company; https://www.pbs.org/wgbh/americanexperience/features/tcrr-timeline/; https://www.up.com/timeline/index.cfm/breaking-ground; https://en.wikipedia.org/wiki/Union_Pacific_Center ; https://www.up.com/timeline/index.cfm/new-up-headquarters

**Goose Hollow**

Larsen, Lawrence, Cottrell, Dalstrom, and Calame Dalstrom. Upstream Metropolis: An Urban Biography of Omaha & Council Bluffs. University of Nebraska Press, 2007.; Otis, Harry B. with Donald Erickson. E Pluribus Omaha: Immigrants All. Lamplighter Press: 2000. *Omaha Daily Bee* August 20, 1917; August 21, 1917. https://www.amidsummersmural.com/south-omaha-mural-project trashed/croatian-mural-proje ct/; https://stspeterpaulomaha.org/parish-history/

**Cut-Off Island**

http://www.cityofcarterlake.com/history; https://en.wikipedia.org/wiki/Carter_Lake,_Iowa; *Omaha World-Herald*. "What's the deal with Carter Lake?" June 29, 2018.; "Court decision allows Carter Lake casino to stay open" August 14, 2019.

**Hummel Park**

https://northomahahistory.com/2015/10/28/the-reality-of-ghosts-at-hummel-park/; https://en.wikipedia.org/wiki/Hummel_Park; *Omaha Magazine*. "The History and Mystery of Hummel Park" October 31, 2018. https://en.wikipedia.org/wiki/Fort_Lisa_(Nebraska); https://en.wikipedia.org/wiki/Cabanne%27s_Trading_Post

**A German Prince and George Washington**

http://bigmuddyworkshop.com/our-work/historic-preservation/mount-vernon-gardens.php ; https://en.wikipedia.org/wiki/Prince_Maximilian_of_Wied-Neuwied; https://www.visitomaha.com/listings/mount-vernon-gardens/57082/; http://plainshumanities.unl.edu/encyclopedia/doc/egp.ea.027; https://en.wikipedia.org/wiki/Karl_Bodmer; http://nebraskarealtyonline.com/our-community/mount-vernon-gardens-omaha-nebraska/

**The Original Omaha**

http://www.e-nebraskahistory.org/index.php?title=Nebraska_Historical_Marker:_Before_Creigh t on; https://en.wikipedia.org/wiki/Gene_Leahy_Mall; *Omaha World-Herald* "A brief history of Omaha's Gene Leahy mall" June 13, 2018. "Omaha says goodbye to old Gene Leahy mall." March 1, 2019.; https://riverfrontrevitalization.com/; https://assets.simpleviewinc.com/simpleview/image/upload/v1/clients/omaha/Public_Art_Walking_Tour2_25a31af0-07cb-4ac9-979b-129bb49a11de.pdf

**Only Governor for Two Days**

*Lincoln Journal Star*. "Bellevue's historic buildings among Nebraska's oldest" May 13, 2012. *Omaha Magazine*. "Francis Burt" October 28, 2018. http://sarpycountymuseum.org/2016/08/the-fontenelle-bank/; http://sarpycountymuseum.org/explore/; "La Velle Vue" Studies in the History of Bellevue Nebraska. Edited by Jerold L. Simmons. Walsworth Publishing, 1976.; https://en.wikipedia.org/wiki/Log_Cabin_(Bellevue,_Nebraska)

**The Golden Spike**

Warner, Dr. Richard, and Ryan Roenfeld. *Council Bluffs*. Arcadia Publishing, 2014. https://en.wikipedia.org/wiki/Union_Pacific_(film); https://www.nps.gov/gosp/learn/historyculture/four-special-spikes.htm; http://www.uprrmuseum.org/uprrm/; https://www.barrescueupdates.com/2014/03/bar-rescue-oface-bar-update.html

**The General in a Garden**

https://www.nps.gov/people/george-crook.htm; https://www.battlefields.org/learn/biographies/george-crook ; https://www.pbs.org/weta/thewest/people/a_c/crook.htm; https://northomahahistory.com/2015/10/07/a-history-of-fort-omaha/; https://en.wikipedia.org/wiki/George_Crook; http://douglascohistory.net/visit.html

**Site of Courtland Beach**
*Daily Nonpareil*. "Carter Lakes colorful, confusing history" August 27, 2012. *Omaha Daily Bee*. "Omaha's Resort" June 17, 1893.; "How Omaha Celebrated" July 5, 1895. https://en.wikipedia.org/wiki/Carter_Lake_(Iowa%E2%80%93Nebraska); https://northomahahistory.com/2016/03/27/a-history-of-north-omahas-municipal-beach-on-carter-lake/; https://northomahahistory.com/2018/04/27/a-history-of-omahas-cortland-beach/; https://en.wikipedia.org/wiki/Carter_Lake_(Iowa%E2%80%93Nebraska)

**The Military Road**
*Lincoln Journal Star*. "Jim McKee: From trails to Nebraska's military roads, highways and interstate" May 18, 2012.; *Omaha Bee*. "Douglas County has many miles of paved highways" April 2, 1911. "Revolving fund will speed up Omaha paving" April 15, 1921.; Franzwa, Gregory. *Maps of the California Trail*. Patrice Press, 1999. ; https://en.wikipedia.org/wiki/Military_Road_(Omaha); https://enacademic.com/dic.nsf/enwiki/8065561

**ASARCO**
*Lincoln Journal Star*. "'Labor' sculpture reflects Omaha's work history." October 9, 2004.; https://en.wikipedia.org/wiki/Asarco; http://memories.ne.gov/cdm/singleitem/collection/opl/id/259/rec/12; https://steppingintothemap.com/anthropocene/items/show/9; https://en.wikipedia.org/wiki/Lewis_and_Clark_Landing; https://www.nps.gov/lecl/planyourvisit/lecl_headquarters.htm

**California Street**
*Daily Nonpareil*. "More Improvements" July 19, 1887.; April 20, 1889.; Davis, Oscar F. *Map of Omaha City, Nebraska* (1866). *Omaha Daily Bee* April 10, 1917; July 4, 1920.; https://northomahahistory.com/2019/12/04/a-history-of-creighton-university/ ; https://en.wikipedia.org/wiki/Morrison_Stadium; https://www.stjohns-creighton.org/history-1; https://www.dicon.com/projects/creighton-california-street-mall/; https://en.wikipedia.org/wiki/Creighton_University

**Lowering the Streets**
*Lincoln Journal Star*. "Omaha was a tough town to pave" December 29, 2018. *Omaha Daily Bee*. June 28, 1903.; August 5, 1906.; August 31, 1919.; *Omaha World-Herald*. "In early Omaha the hills had to go for the city to grow" May 8, 2018. "Omaha's St. Mary Magdalene has met its share of challenges over 150 years." May 30, 2017.; Orr, Richard. *O&CB: Streetcars of Omaha and Council Bluffs*. Richard Orr, 1996.; https://stmarymagdaleneomaha.org/

**The Florence Mill**
*Omaha Bee*. January 2, 1906. https://en.wikipedia.org/wiki/Florence_Mill_(Omaha,_Nebraska); http://www.historicflorence.org/PublicArt/birth-of-the-west.php; Nomination to the National Register of Historic Places. Weber Mill. www.npsgallery.nps.gov; http://www.historicomaha.com/flrncmil.htm

**Omaha's Exposition and Indian Congress**
*Omaha Bee*. "Plan for Indian Congress" April 10, 1898. https://en.wikipedia.org/wiki/Trans-Mississippi_Exposition; http://trans-mississippi.unl.edu/ https://en.wikipedia.org/wiki/Indian_Congress; https://northomahahistory.com/2015/10/09/a-history-of-omahas-greater-america-exposition-of-1899/; https://en.wikipedia.org/wiki/Frederic_Thompson

**Winter Quarters**
Boughter, Judith A. *Betraying the Omaha Nation 1790-1916*. University of Oklahoma Press, 1998.; https://history.churchofjesuschrist.org/article/trek/winter-quarters; https://northomahahistory.com/2016/05/27/a-history-of-the-mormon-tree-formerly-in-the-florence-park-in-north-omaha/; https://history.nebraska.gov/blog/omahas-tragedy-winter-quarters-monument; https://www.waymarking.com/waymarks/wm1VR3_Winter_Quarters_Florence_City_Park

**The Greektown Riot**
*Daily Nonpareil.* "Enraged Greek kills officer" February 20, 1909. "Aroused against Greeks" February 21, 1909.; *Omaha Bee.* "King of Greece can only demand damages" February 26, 1909. https://www.pappaspost.com/on-this-day-february-21-1909-anti-greek-riot-in-south-omaha/; https://en.wikipedia.org/wiki/Greek_Town_riot; https://history.nebraska.gov/blog/anti-greek-riot-1909; *Lincoln Star Journal* "Omaha's 'Plaza de la Raza' could be a tourist attraction" March 3, 2004.; https://www.amidsummersmural.com/south-omaha-mural-project trashed/the-plaza-de-la-raza-mural-project/

**The Prague Hotel**
*Lincoln Journal Star.* "Czech immigrants shaped state" August 11, 2018. *Omaha Daily Bee.* Advertisement. December 10, 1898; Menard, Orville. *River City Empire: Tom Dennison's Omaha.* University of Nebraska Press, 1989.; Miller, Linda. *Omaha: A Guide to the City and Environs.* Compiled by WPA. Omaha Public Library, 1981.; https://en.wikipedia.org/wiki/Edward_Rosewater; https://en.wikipedia.org/wiki/Prague_Hotel; https://en.wikipedia.org/wiki/Little_Bohemia_(Omaha,_Nebraska)

**A Pabst Tied House**
*Omaha Daily Bee.* "South Omaha News" February 27, 1899. https://en.wikipedia.org/wiki/Pabst_Brewing_Company; https://en.wikipedia.org/wiki/Pabst_Blue_Ribbon; https://restorationexchange.org/2017/07/27/pabst-schlitz-omahas-saloon-history/; Project QU-515(8) A Relocation Study. Nebraska Department of Roads, 1972. https://www.visitomaha.com/restaurants/breweries/

**Scars of the 1919 Courthouse Riot**
*Omaha World-Herald.* "Douglas County Courthouse murals have a colorful past." April 24, 2017.; Menard, Dr. Orville. *River City Empire: Tom Dennison's Omaha.* University of Nebraska Press, 1989.; https://en.wikipedia.org/wiki/Douglas_County_Courthouse_(Nebraska); https://en.wikipedia.org/wiki/John_Latenser_Sr. ; https://en.wikipedia.org/wiki/Omaha_race_riot_of_1919

**Brandeis**
*Omaha Daily Bee.* Advertisement. December 6, 1908. https://en.wikipedia.org/wiki/J._L._Brandeis_and_Sons; https://en.wikipedia.org/wiki/J._L._Brandeis_and_Sons_Store_Building; https://www.geni.com/people/Jonas-Brandeis/6000000013705200266; *Washington Post.* "Blumkin: Sofa, So good." May 24, 1984.

**Potter's Field**
http://www.historicflorence.org/Cemeteries/PottersCemeterySiteX4.php; https://en.wikipedia.org/wiki/Potter%27s_Field_(Omaha) *Omaha Daily Bee.* February 4, 1889. https://www.ketv.com/article/all-the-people-here-deserve-it-volunteers-clean-potters-field-will-brown-memorial/28884225; https://en.wikipedia.org/wiki/Anne_Ramsey

**The Otoe Mission**
Merrill, Moses, Rev., *Wdwdklha Tva Eva Wdhonetl* in 1834. https://history.nebraska.gov/collections/moses-merrill-1803-1840-rg2242am; Wishart, David J. *An Unspeakable Sadness: The Dispossession of the Nebraska Indians.* University of Nebraska Press, 1994. https://en.wikipedia.org/wiki/Moses_Merrill_Mission; https://www.omtribe.org/who-we-are-history ; https://www.traillink.com/trail/bellevue-loop-trail/

**Omaha's Main Street**
Johnson, Harrison. *Johnson's History of Nebraska.* H. Gibson, 1880. *Omaha Daily Bee.* "Our Elkhorn Letter" April 30, 1874. http://www.kancoll.org/books/andreas_ne/douglas/douglas-p55.html; http://cprr.org/Museum/Silvis/ https://en.wikipedia.org/wiki/Elkhorn,_Omaha,_Nebraska https://www.oldetowneelkhorn.org/; https://sites.google.com/site/elkhornhistory/important-dates-in-elkhorn-history; https://www.unomaha.edu/college-of-public-affairs-and-community-service/center-for-public-aff ai rs-research/documents/nebraska-historical-population-report-2018.pdf; https://en.wikipedia.org/wiki/Lincoln_Highway_(Omaha)

**The Blockhouse and Mission**
Clifton, James A. *The Prairie People: Continuity and Change in Potawatomi Indian Culture, 1665-1965*. University of Iowa Press, 1998.; http://fortwiki.com/Council_Bluffs_Blockhouse https://en.wikipedia.org/wiki/Pierre-Jean_De_Smet; De Smet, Pierre Jean. *Life, Letters, and Travels of Father Pierre-Jean De Smet, S.J.: 1801-1873*. F.P. Harper, 1905. https://en.wikipedia.org/wiki/100_Block_of_West_Broadway_Historic_District; https://www.unleashcb.com/play/place/historic_100_block_of_west_broadway/

**DeBolt**
*Omaha Daily Bee*. "Sheriff Clark firm stand on hog nuisance" July 20, 1919. Morton, Julius Sterling. *An Illustrated History of Nebraska*. J. North, 1913. https://northomahahistory.com/2017/03/19/a-history-of-debolt/; http://graveyardsofomaha.com/springwell/springwell_main.html; https://en.wikipedia.org/wiki/Springwell_Danish_Cemetery; http://www.mangiaitaliana.com/menu; https://en.wikipedia.org/wiki/Cowboy_Trail

**Monuments to Stockyards**
*Omaha Daily Bee*. "Stockyards here grow in 40 years to second in U.S." June 19, 1921; http://netnebraska.org/basic-page/television/beef-state-omaha-stockyards; https://en.wikipedia.org/wiki/Union_Stockyards_(Omaha); https://en.wikipedia.org/wiki/South_Omaha_Land_Company; https://livinghistoryfarm.org/farminginthe50s/money_14.html

**The Iowa School for the Deaf**
https://www.iowaschoolforthedeaf.org/find-out-more/history/; *Daily Nonpareil*. "Iowa School for the Deaf celebrates its history." September 24, 2013; https://en.wikipedia.org/wiki/Iowa_School_for_the_Deaf; https://en.wikipedia.org/wiki/American_Sign_Language; Nickens, Carol J. *The History of American Sign Language* "A.S.L." Lulu, 2008. https://en.wikipedia.org/wiki/Nebraska_School_for_the_Deaf https://www.wabashtrace.org/

**Depot on the Omaha Road**
*Omaha Daily Bee*. "A Bastardy case" July 21, 1887.; Orr, Richard. *O&CB: Streetcars of Omaha and Council Bluffs*. Richard Orr, 1996.; Savage, James Woodruff, John Thomas Bell, and Consul Willshire Butterfield. *History of the City of Omaha, Nebraska*. Munsell, 1894. http://www.historicflorence.org/Attractions/depot.php; https://en.wikipedia.org/wiki/Florence_Depot; https://en.wikipedia.org/wiki/Chicago,_St._Paul,_Minneapolis_and_Omaha_Railway; https://www.cnwhs.org/ch_spmo.htm; https://northomahahistory.com/2016/12/08/j-j-pershing-drive-and-monument/

**The Gangster and the Architect**
*Omaha Daily Bee*. "Midway owners indicted" February 14, 1912 "Jack Broomfield is sued for divorce" September 11, 1921.; Menard, Orville. *River City Empire: Tom Dennison's Omaha*. University of Nebraska Press: 1989.; https://en.wikipedia.org/wiki/Broomfield_Rowhouse ; https://en.wikipedia.org/wiki/Clarence_W._Wigington ; https://northomahahistory.com/2016/07/08/a-short-history-of-the-24th-and-lake-historic-district- in-north-omaha-nebraska/95a3c-broomfield2browhouse/; https://northomahahistory.com/2016/07/14/a-short-history-of-crime-bosses-in-north-omaha-ne br aska/; https://en.wikipedia.org/wiki/Zion_Baptist_Church_(Omaha,_Nebraska)

**Marker for the Mainline**
Bangs, S.D. "History of Sarpy County." *Publications Nebraska State Historical Society, Volume II*, 1887.; Johnson, Harrison. *Johnson's History of Nebraska*. H. Gibson, 1880. https://en.wikipedia.org/wiki/Papillion,_Nebraska; https://www.up.com/timeline/index.cfm/lane-cutoff https://en.wikipedia.org/wiki/Thomas_C._Durant; https://en.wikipedia.org/wiki/Cr%C3%A9dit_Mobilier_scandal; https://www.up.com/timeline/index.cfm/lane-cutoff http://www.papillion-ahs.com/

**Ak-Sar-Ben Air Field**
https://en.wikipedia.org/wiki/Ak-Sar-Ben_(arena) https://history.nebraska.gov/blog/marker-monday-ak-sar-ben-field-and-us-air-mail http://www.airfields-freeman.com/NE/Airfields_NE_NE.htm; https://www.historynet.com/great-transcontinental-air-race.htm https://en.wikipedia.org/wiki/Maha_Music_Festival https://en.wikipedia.org/wiki/Omaha_(horse)

**Futurism, Bicycles, and Coffee**
https://en.wikipedia.org/wiki/Old_Post_Office_(Omaha,_Nebraska)
*New York Times*. "The End of 1960's Architecture" October 31, 2004. http://www. thebikeunion. org/; *Omaha World-Herald*. "Vacant 'saucer' near 19th and Dodge set to become bike shop, job training site. February 23, 2015.; "Downtown building's distinctive design is from the 1960s, not Mars" March 25, 2015.; *Omaha Magazine*. "The Flying Saucer on Dodge Street." August 25, 2016.

**Cutler's Park**
Jorgensen, Danny L. "The Cutlerites of Southwestern Iowa: A Latter-day Saint Schism and Its Role in the Early Settlement of Iowa." The Annals of Iowa, Spring 1999.; https://www. historicflorence.org/HistoricMarkers/CutlersParkMarker.php http://www.allaboutomaha.com/ HistoricFlorence/Mormons/CutlersPark.php; https://en.wikipedia.org/wiki/Alpheus_Cutler; https://www.deseret.com/1997/4/26/20771606/roadside-park-opened-at-site-of-nebraska-s-firs t- city; http://winterquarters.byu.edu/settlements/nebraska.html; *Valley News*. "Manti Park to honor the past." October 10, 2008.

**Resting Place of the Omaha Kid**
https://catholiccem.com/cemeteries/stmarys/ https://boxrec.com/; *Indianapolis Times*. June 6, 1924.; *Lake County Times*. December 11, 1920.; *Omaha Daily Bee*. July 6, 1906.; "Mrs. Mary Kilker dies at 87 years" February 10, 1916. September 12, 1918; November 21, 1919.; April 3, 1921.; January 5, 1922.; February 18, 1922.; June 13, 1922.; https://www.findagrave.com/ cemetery/101352/saint-mary's-cemetery; http://lithuanianbakery.biz/

**The Byron Reed Numismatics**
Sorenson, Alfred Rasmus. *Omaha Illustrated*. D.C. Dunbar, 1888. https://en.wikipedia.org/ wiki/Byron_Reed_Collection; https://dataomaha.com/bigstory/story/117/living/byron-reed-collection-a-rare-peek-at-omahas-t re asure; https://preferredcoinexchange.com/2018/06/28/ museums-every-numismatist-must-visit/; https://durhammuseum.org/; *Omaha World-Herald*. "Durham museum opens rarely seen basement vaults." April 10, 2018. https://en.wikipedia.org/ wiki/Union_Station_(Omaha) https://www.byronreedcompany.com/

**Mr. Blandings's Dream Home**
https://en.wikipedia.org/wiki/Mr._Blandings_Builds_His_Dream_House; https://www.ketv.com/ article/restored-dream-house-with-classic-film-ties-hits-the-market-in-om a ha/32197806#; https://myomahaobsession.com/2020/03/23/mysteries-of-omaha-the-mr-blandings-dream-hou se/; *Omaha World-Herald*. "The homes where Omaha's stars got their start" June 8, 2013.; "In 1948, an Omaha dream house was built and raffled." March 28, 2018.; https://en.wikipedia. org/wiki/Marlon_Brando

**The Singing Tower of Westlawn**
*Omaha Daily Bee*. August 29, 1915.; October 18, 1918.; November 10, 1918.; May 11, 1919.; "Cemetery Notes." *Park and Cemetery and Landscape Gardening*. R.J. Haight, 1914. https:// www.findagrave.com/cemetery/101611/westlawn-hillcrest-memorial-park ; http://www. graveyardsofomaha.com/westlawn/westlawn_main.html ; https://en.wikipedia.org/wiki/ Westlawn-Hillcrest_Funeral_Home_and_Memorial_Park; http://www.e-nebraskahistory.org/ index.php?title=Fred_A._Henninger,_Jr._(1897-1991),_Architect; "The Singing Tower." Undated postcard. Eric Nelson News Company, Omaha. https://dot.nebraska.gov/travel/map-library/; https://en.wikipedia.org/wiki/U.S._Route_6_in_Nebraska; Wakeley, Arthur Cooper. *Omaha: the Gate City, and Douglas County, Nebraska, Volume II*. S.J. Clarke, 1917. https://www.npdodge. com/history/

**Everything at the Center**
*Daily Nonpareil* December 20, 1953.; *Omaha World-Herald*. October 25, 1955.; June 13, 2004; "As Younkers prepares to to close, Omahans reminisce." April 23, 2018. http://mall-hall-of-fame. blogspot.com/2007/02/center-center-and-south-42nd-streets.html http://mallsofamerica. blogspot.com/2006/01/center-shopping-center.html; https://en.wikipedia.org/wiki/Westroads_ Mal; https://en.wikipedia.org/wiki/Better_Call_Saul; https://www.cinnabon.com/ne

**Last Home of the Tong**
*Omaha World-Herald*. "Former hub for Omaha's Chinese community recognized as historic place" October 16, 2019.; *Omaha Magazine*. "Chinatown lost and found" March 2, 2018. https://www.omahamagazine.com/2018/04/03/302077/a-revolutionary-meeting ; https://northomahahistory.com/2019/03/05/a-history-of-omahas-chinatown-by-ryan-roenfeld/; https://en.wikipedia.org/wiki/On_Leong_Chinese_Merchants_Association; https://panda-house.com/

**The *Tägliche Omaha Tribüne***
Otis, Harry B. with Donald H. Erickson. *E Pluribus Omaha: Immigrants All*. Lamplighter Press, 2000.; Wakeley, Arthur Cooper. *Omaha, the Gate City, and Douglas County, Nebraska, Volume II*. S.J. Clarke, 1917.; https://en.wikipedia.org/wiki/Valentin_J._Peter https://en.wikipedia.org/wiki/German_American_journalism; *Omaha Daily Bee*. November 15, 1915.; April 21, 1918.; April 27, 1918. https://www.findagrave.com/memorial/141745326/valentine-joseph-peter; https://history.nebraska.gov/blog/nebraska-digital-newspaper-program-earns-200000-grant

**Gibson**
*Daily Nonpareil* March 17, 1901; October 15, 1901; July 30, 1904; *Omaha Bee*. May 24, 1913.; July 9, 1922.; July 23, 1923.; August 26, 1923. ; https://en.wikipedia.org/wiki/Omaha_station_(Chicago,_Burlington_and_Quincy_Railroad); https://en.wikipedia.org/wiki/Gibson_Bend; https://en.wikipedia.org/wiki/Omaha_Zoo_Railroad; http://www.elmuseolatino.org/index.php; https://www.census.gov/quickfacts/omahacitynebraska

**Home of an Ice Baron**
https://en.wikipedia.org/wiki/John_P._Bay_House; https://landmark.cityofomaha.org/article/4035-john-p-bay-residence; https://northomahahistory.com/2015/06/15/a-history-of-mansions-and-estates-in-north-omaha/ *Omaha Daily Bee* February 16, 1886.; January 23, 1889.; January 24, 1889.; March 4, 1894.; September 21, 1902.; February 6, 1916.; December 17, 1916 https://en.wikipedia.org/wiki/Kountze_Place

**Druid Hall**
*Omaha Daily Bee*. April 25, 1915.; Omaha Guide. December 4, 1937. https://landmark.cityofomaha.org/article/7959-druid-hall; https://en.wikipedia.org/wiki/Joseph_P._Guth https://nebraskagrandlodge.wordpress.com/2015/04/12/prince-hall-masons-celebrate-the-100t h- birthday-of-druid-hall/; https://en.wikipedia.org/wiki/Prince_Hall_Freemasonry; https://en.wikipedia.org/wiki/Scottish_Rite_Cathedral_(Omaha,_Nebraska)

**Site of the St. Nicholas**
*Omaha Daily Bee*. January 10, 1909. https://en.wikipedia.org/wiki/Kansas%E2%80%93Nebraska_Act; https://en.wikipedia.org/wiki/Lone_Tree_Ferry; https://en.wikipedia.org/wiki/St._Nicholas_Hotel_(Omaha,_Nebraska); Sorenson, Alfred Rasmus. *History of Omaha from the Pioneer Days to the Present Time*. Gibson, Miller & Richardson, 1889.; https://www.hollywoodcandy.com/

**The Last of Jobber's Canyon**
*Omaha Daily Bee*. November 18, 1905. *Omaha World-Herald*. "$500 million revamp of old Conagra campus officially underway" March 2, 2020; https://en.wikipedia.org/wiki/Nash_Block ; https://en.wikipedia.org/wiki/Jobbers_Canyon_Historic_District; https://landmark.cityofomaha.org/article/4050-nash-block-mckesson-robbins-warehouse; https://en.wikipedia.org/wiki/Old_Market_(Omaha,_Nebraska) ; https://en.wikipedia.org/wiki/Burlington_Headquarters_Building

**Omaha's First Skyscraper**
*Omaha Daily Bee*. February 5, 1888.; January 10, 1910.; Gerber, Kristine. *Omaha and Council Bluffs: Yesterday and Today*. Nonpareil Publishing, 2008. https://en.wikipedia.org/wiki/List_of_tallest_buildings_in_the_United_States; https://en.wikipedia.org/wiki/List_of_tallest_buildings_in_Omaha,_Nebraska; https://en.wikipedia.org/wiki/Omaha_National_Bank_Building; *Omaha World-Herald*. "Omaha's tallest buildings" February 3, 2019. https://en.wikipedia.org/wiki/First_National_Bank_Tower; https://www.trekupthetower.org/; https://en.wikipedia.org/wiki/WoodmenLife_Tower; https://www.omahamagazine.com/2019/09/26/301117/art-architecture-and-a-historic-treasure

**The Farmers Home**

https://en.wikipedia.org/wiki/Ezra_Millard; *Omaha Daily Bee*. June 16, 1887.; July 2, 1905.; August 24, 1912. https://en.wikipedia.org/wiki/Millard,_Omaha,_Nebraska; https://archive.org/details/ReconnaissanceLevelSurveyForMillard; *Omaha World-Herald*. "Rebirth: Site of former Western Electric plant has been transformed" February 2, 2014.; "Nightlife review: With scores of TVs and craft beers…" August 17, 2019. https://cdm16747.contentdm.oclc.org/digital/collection/p16747coll3/id/12/rec/3; http://www.localbeer.co/millard; http://www.millarddays.com/

**A Park for Survivors**

https://parks.cityofomaha.org/park-details?pid=11; *Onocology Times*. "Cancer Survivors Parks Now in 20 cities" February 25, 2004.; http://blochcancer.org/about/cancer-survivors-parks/; https://en.wikipedia.org/wiki/Regency_(Omaha); https://kcparks.org/places/bloch-cancer-survivors-park/; https://en.wikipedia.org/wiki/Richard_Bloch; https://en.wikipedia.org/wiki/Cancer,_There_Is_Hope

**Big Elk**

Boughter, Judith A. *Betraying the Omaha Nation 1790-1916*. University of Oklahoma Press, 1998.; Simmons, Jerold L., editor. "La Belle Vue": *Studies in the History of Bellevue, Nebraska*. Walsworth Publishing, 1976.; http://graveyardsofomaha.com/bellevue; https://www.findagrave.com/memorial/11431/big_elk-ong-pa-ton-ga; https://en.wikipedia.org/wiki/Big_Elk; https://nebraskahistory.pastperfectonline.com/byperson?keyword=Big+Elk; https://history.nebraska.gov/sites/history.nebraska.gov/files/doc/publications/NH2014BigElk.pdf; https://blogs.bellevue.edu/library/index.php/2017/03/nebraska-history-the-original-bellevue-coll e ge/; *Omaha World-Herald*. June 15, 2020

**Hell's Half Acre**

Larsen, Lawrence, Barbara J. Cottrell Dalstrom, Harl Dalstrom, Kay Calame Dalstrom. *Upstream Metropolis: An Urban Biography of Omaha & Council Bluffs*. University of Nebraska Press, 2007.; Roenfeld, Ryan. *Wicked Omaha*. History Press, 2017.; Washburn, Josie. *The Underworld Sewer: A Prostitute Reflects on Life in the Trade, 1871-1909*. University of Nebraska Press, 1997. https://capitoldistrictomaha.com/

**Dundee Streetcars**

*Omaha Daily Bee*. July 31, 1887.; August 28, 1887.; September 3, 1889.; December 9, 1894.; *Omaha World-Herald*. "Celebrating Omaha's small but vital Jewish community" September 8, 2014.; https://www.dundee-memorialpark.org/history-architecture; https://en.wikipedia.org/wiki/Dundee%E2%80%93Happy_Hollow_Historic_District; https://www.dundeegarden.org/

**Around the World to Omaha**

Bossier Banner. January 6, 1872.; *Daily State Register*. September 4, 1872.; *Daily Nonpareil*. October 31, 1871; *Omaha Daily Bee*. May 8, 1894.; *Omaha World-Herald*. "Wildly colorful George Francis Train was a key player for the transcontinental railroad." December 13, 2017; https://history.nebraska.gov/publications/train-george-francis; https://www.newenglandhistoricalsociety.com/george-francis-train-one-of-few-sane-men-mad- m ad-world/; https://en.wikipedia.org/wiki/George_Francis_Train; https://www.americanheritage.com/faces-past-x ; https://en.wikipedia.org/wiki/Credit_Foncier_of_America; https://en.wikipedia.org/wiki/George_P._Bemis; https://en.wikipedia.org/wiki/Bemis_Park_Landmark_Heritage_District ; https://en.wikipedia.org/wiki/Dahlman_neighborhood

# INDEX

Aeppli, Eva, 8–9

Ak-Sar-Ben, 14–15, 20, 144, 167

Ak-Sar-Ben Field, 144–145

Allen's Showcase, 2

Allwine, Antoinette, 36

Allwine, Arthur, 36

Alston, Littleton, 2

Andersen Park, 176

ASARCO, 84

Bagel, 185

Balcom, Jake, 5

Bay, John P., 166

Beadle, Erastus, 46–47

Bear Shield, 58

Beckwith, Captain Edward, 82

Bellevue, Nebraska, 60–61, 69, 74–75, 79, 123, 126–127, 143, 158, 180–181

Bellevue cemetery, 180–181

Bellevue Loop Trail, 126

Bemis, George, 186–187

Bemis Park, 186

Benson, 1, 28–29, 82

Benson, Erastus, 28

Benson & Halcyon Heights Street Railway, 28

Bere's Hall, 65

Big Elk, Chief, 148, 180–181

Big Papio Trail, 46, 179

Bike Union and Coffee, 147

Bloody Corner, 32–33

Blumkin, Rose, 122

Bodmer, Karl, 70

Borglum, Gutzon, 42

Bouguereau, William-Adolphe, 42

Brandeis, Jonas, 122–123

Brando, Marlon, 154

Breese, Lillian, 114

Broadview Hotel, 35

Broomfield, Jack, 140–141

Brown, William, 120, 124–125

Burlington railroad, 164, 173

Burt, Francis, 74–75

Cabanne, Jean Pierre, 69

Caldwell, Billy, 130–131

California Street, 73, 86–87

Cancer Survivors Park, 178–179

Caniglia, Grazia Bonafede, 5

Capitol District, 182

Capitol Hill, 26–27

Carlentini, Sicily, 4

Carnation ballroom, 2

Carter, Levi, 80–81

Carter Lake, Iowa, 66, 80–81, 167

Center Mall, 158

Central Elementary School, 26–27

Chambers, Ernie, 86

Cheyenne, 16, 79, 126

Chez Paree, 66

CHI Health Center, 6, 63

Chinatown, 160–161

Cinnabon, 158

Civic Auditorium, 6–7

Cleveland, H.W.S., 34

Cold Springs Camp, 148

ConAgra, 173

Council Bluffs, Iowa, 1, 18–20, 66, 67, 68, 74, 75–77, 113, 115, 131, 136, 145, 155, 157, 170

Council Bluffs Blockhouse, 130–131

Courtland Beach, 80–81

Creedon, P.J., 86

Creighton University, 73, 86–87

Crook, General George, 78–79

Crossroads, 123

Cuming, Thomas, 41, 60, 74–75

Cutler, Alpheus, 148–149

Cutler's Park, 148–149

Cut-Off Island, 66

Dahlman, Jim, 120, 162

Dahlman Park, 187

Danish American Society, 50

Danish Brotherhood, 50–51

Dargaczewski, Nicodemus, 57

Darling, Dick, 46

Daub, Hal, 29

DeBolt, 132–133

Dennison, Ada, 35

Dennison, Tom, 35, 44–45, 57, 68, 116, 120, 140–141

De Smet, Pierre-Jean, 130–131

Dinker's Bar, 57

di Suvero, Mark, 20

Dodds, Everett S., 49

Dodge, General Grenville, 142

Douglas County, Nebraska, 57, 114, 120–121, 132

Dreamland ballroom, 2

Dreamland Plaza, 2

Druid Hall, 168–169

Dundee, 1, 10–11, 13, 64, 128, 132, 184–185

Dundee Place, 184

Durant, Dr. Thomas, 142, 186

East Omaha, 66–67, 80

Elkhorn, 34, 128–129, 132, 133, 180

El Museo Latino, 164

Elmwood Park, 53

Enron, 26

Fairbanks, Avard, 112

Farmers Home Hotel, 176–177

First National Tower, 174

Fisher, George, 166

Florence, 1, 13, 34, 60–61, 108–109, 138–139

Florence Bank, 60–61

Florence Boulevard, 34–35, 111

Florence Depot, 138–139

Florence Field, 48

Florence Mill, 108–109

Ford, President Gerald R., 44

Forest Lawn Cemetery, 124

Fort Atkinson, 68, 180

Fort Calhoun, Nebraska, 68

Fort Crook, 79, 145

Fort Lisa, 68–69

Fort Omaha, 34, 78–79

Frank Stoysich Meats, 56

Fremont, Elkhorn & Missouri Valley railroad, 34, 132–133

French, Daniel Chester, 18

French Cafe, 9

Fry, Thomas A., 166–167

Gallagher, Rachel, 39, 52

Garden of the Zodiac, 8

German-American Society, 24–25

Geronimo, 79, 111

Gibson, 164–165

Glacier Creek, 36–37

Golden Spike, 76–77

Goodkind, Terry, 29

Goose Hollow, 64

Grand Encampment, 137

Great Plains Black History Museum, 2

Greektown, 114–115

Hanscom Park, 44–45, 56

Hartong, Clinton, 32

Heaney Pedestrian Bridge, 87

Hell Creek, 58

Hell On Wheels, 62, 142

Hell's Half Acre, 182

Henninger, Fred A. Jr., 157

Henry Doorly Zoo, 24, 165

Highway 6, 20

Hollywood Candy, 170–171

Holy Sepulchre Cemetery, 40–41

Hood, George, 70

Hummel Park, 68–69

Ietan, Chief, 127

Indian Congress, 110

Indian Hills, 147

Interstate 480, 20, 57

Iowa School for the Deaf, 136–137

Jobber's Canyon, 172

Joslyn Art Museum, 42–43, 70

Kaminski, Stanislaus, 56–57

Keith, Miguel Lance Corp., 32

Kennedy Freeway, 118

Keystone Trail, 53

Kimball, Thomas, 22–23, 140, 172–173

Kipling, Rudyard, 32

Kountze Place, 54, 166

Krug, Frederick, 38

Krug Park, 38–39, 81

Kutak Rock law firm, 175

Lake Manawa, 81, 150

Lapidus, Harry, 44–45

Latenser, John Sr., 26, 107, 120, 122

Latenser, Nes, 146

Lawler, Jack, 150–151

Leahy, Eugene, 13

Lentini, Sicily

Leonov, Alexei, 121

Levi Carter Park, 81

Lewis and Clark, 68, 71–72, 84

Lincoln, Abraham, 18, 62, 76

Lincoln, Nebraska, 26, 140, 156, 163

Lincoln Highway, 18, 20–21, 30, 128, 156

Lininger, George, 42–43

Lisa, Manuel, 48, 68

Lithuanian Bakery, 151

Livestock Exchange Building, 134–135

Loess Hills, 18

Love's Jazz Center, 2

Lowrey, Ed, 114

Lumberyard District, 177

Mackay, James, 72

Maha Music Festival, 144

Malcolm X, 6

Malec brothers, 30

Mancusco Music Hall, 6

Mandan Park, 71

Mangia Italiana, 132

Martin, Charles, 48–49

Masourides, John, 114–115

Maximilian of Wied-Nuewied, Prince, 70–71

McKim, Mead, and White, 22, 174

Meigs, Linda, 109

Memorial Park, 11, 185

Mercer, Sam, 8–9

Mercer, Sam Dr., 8–9

Merrill, Eliza, 126

Merrill, Moses, 126–127

Metropolitan Cable Railway, 184–185

Mickells, Nicholas, 64

Mignery, Herb, 73

Military Avenue, 1, 28, 82

Military Road, 28, 38, 82–83

Millard, 1, 12–13, 58, 128, 132, 143, 176

Millard, Ezra, 176

Millard Heights Park, 12

Mill Creek, 108, 148

Miller Park, 34, 48, 49

Minne Lusa, 48–49

Missouri River, 1, 18, 21, 26, 46, 66, 68–70, 72, 75, 80, 84–85, 112–113, 124, 126, 148, 150, 164, 170, 173, 180, 182, 187

Mitchell, James, 60

Mormon Battalion, 137

Mt. Vernon Gardens, 70–71, 89

*Mr. Blandings Builds His Dream House*, 154

Nash Block, 172–173

National Register of Historic Places, 10, 19, 23, 48, 51, 83, 108, 117, 123, 131, 161, 168, 172

Nebraska Territory, 41, 46–47, 60–61, 74, 171

Nevins, Carolyn, 54–55

New York Life Insurance Company, 174–175

Niobrara River, 58

Nolte, Nick, 29

Northern Natural Gas, 26

Offutt Air Force Base, 79

Old Market, 1, 8, 119

O-L-D Route, 156

Olympic Cycles, 177

Omaha & Council Bluffs Street Railway, 185

Omaha Central High School, 26

Omaha Platform, 14–15

Omaha Road, 138–139

Omaha Street Railway, 28, 184

On Leong Tong, 160–161

Orsi, Alfonso, 4

Otoe-Missouria Tribe, 127

O Face, 76

O'Neill, John, 40–41

Pabst, Frederick, 118–119

Papillion, Nebraska, 46–47, 142–143

Papillion Creek, 47, 53, 58, 126, 142, 176

Pawnee tribe, 72

Peony Park, 31

People's Party, 14

Pershing, General John J., 34, 68, 139

Peter, Valentin, 162

Pivonka, Joseph, 117

Platte River, 26, 106, 180

Plaza de la Raza, 58, 115

Ponca tribe, 59

Portal School, 143

Potter's Field, 124–125

Prague Hotel, 116–117

Prairie Flower Casino, 66

Presbyterian Mission House, 74

Prinz, George, 134

Ramsey, Anne, 124

Reed, Byron, 152–153

Reed, Robert, 29

Regency, 178

Riverview Park, 24

Rock Brook Farm, 46

Rock Island Railroad, 18

Rosenfield, John, 30

Rosenfield, Karl, 30

Rosewater, Ed, 116

Saints Peter and Paul church, 64–65

Salerno brothers, 4

Salmones, Victor, 179

Santa Lucia, 5

Saratoga, 46, 80

Schiller, Friedrich, 22, 24–25

Scottish Rite Cathedral, 169

Sessinghaus, Edward, 50

Sheelytown, 56–57

Snowden, William and Rachel, 170–171

Sokol Auditorium, 116

Sorenson, Alfred, 72, 152,

South Omaha, 1, 13, 32, 64, 114, 118, 132, 134–135, 150–151

Southside Terrace, 33

Springwell Cemetery, 132

St. Mary Magdalene church, 106–107

St. Mary's Cemetery, 150–151

St. Nicholas hotel, 170–171,

Standing Bear, Chief, 58–59, 79

Standing Bear Lake, 58–59

Stile di Famiglia, 5

Stinson Park, 144

TD Ameritrade, 63

Thompson, William, 16

Tietz, Charles, 38

Tom Hanafan River's Edge Park, 20

Towl Park, 46–47

Train, George Francis, 186

Train Town, 186–187

Trans-Mississippi Exposition, 111

Underwood Hills, 155

Union Pacific Railroad, 4, 8, 12, 16, 20, 62, 63, 77, 84, 142, 143, 168, 176, 186

Union Station, 152, 153

Union Stock Yards, 56

University of Nebraska at Omaha, 52, 55

University of Omaha, 36, 54–55

W. Dale Clark Library, 16–17, 23

Wabash Trace, 136

Waiting Room lounge, 28

Walnut Hill, 28

Wattles, Gurdon, 110

Wavecrest Park, 81

Western Electric, 12, 176–177

Westlawn-Hillcrest cemetery, 156–157

Wiebe, John, 158–159

Wigington, Clarence, 140–141

Williams, Joseph Lee "Big Joe", 2–3

Wilson, 134

Winter Quarters, 60, 108–109, 112–113, 148

WoodmenLife, 174–175

Woodmen of the World, 51

Young, Brigham, 108, 112–113, 148, 149

Younkers, 123, 158

Zaplotnik, John, 64–65

Zion Baptist Church, 141